Traditions of Men
versus
The Word of God

By Alvin Jennings

With Special Section On
The New Testament Church
By L. R. Wilson

D1558775

"Ye leave the _____
hold fast the tradition of men."

— *Jesus Christ*

BIBLE PUBLICATIONS, INC.
An Authorized Non-Profit Organization
7120 BURNS STREET
FORT WORTH, TEXAS 76118

DEDICATION

Dedicated to all those who value their reputation with men less than they value the honor and approval which comes from God (John 12:42b).

First Printing, August, 1972 — 5200
Second Printing, December, 1974 — 5200
Third Printing, March, 1977 — 4000
Fourth Printing, April, 1980 — 50,000
Fifth Printing, October, 1980 — 50,000

"TRADITIONS"

"Traditions" as used in this book are religious laws and regulations originating in the minds of men and handed down orally and/or in printing from generation to generation. Jesus frequently denounced such traditions and warned disciples that following them makes the word of God "of none effect" (see Matthew 15:2, 3, 6; Mark 7:3, 5, 8, 9, 13; Colossians 2:8; 1 Peter 1:18; Galatians 1:14).

"Paradosis" is the Greek word translated tradition. It is defined as that which is given over or handed down by word of mouth or in writing, and can refer to the substance of teaching from whatever source, including the Divine (2 Thessalonians 2:15; 3:6; 1 Corinthians 11:2). This is not the sense in which Jesus used the term in his denunciations, nor is it the way in which it will be used in this book.

TRADITIONS vs WORD of GOD

CONTENTS

PREFACE

It Does Make a Difference What Man Believes and How Man Worships God

The earliest clash between man's idea and God's word in choosing a form of worship is recorded in Genesis 4:2-8. Later, Jude referred to "the way of Cain" (vs. 11) and the apostle John spoke of Cain's wickedness who slew his brother "because his own works were evil, and his brother's righteous" (1 John 3:12). God, in observing Cain's anger and unhappy countenance after he offered the faithless sacrifice, said, "If thou doest well, shalt thou not be accepted? and if thou doest not well, sin lieth at the door" (Genesis 4:7). Cain sinned by transgressing God's law (1 John 3:4), by substituting his own way of worship for God's way. Those who follow in the way of Cain have not learned that God's ways and thoughts are not the same as man's (Isaiah 55:8-9), and that to worship by a form that is pleasing to man will be followed by disastrous consequences. Those who are determined to worship God according to His holy Word will be honored and rewarded like Abel of whom it is said, "By faith Abel offered unto God a more excellent sacrifice than Cain . . ." (Hebrews 11:4). His faith came by hearing God's word (Romans 10:17).

Through the centuries we see man standing with the two ways before him. God's way on the one hand, perhaps appearing narrow and difficult with only a few following. On the other hand, there is the popular way, the broad way, the way that *seems* right to men, but it is the way of death (Jer. 10:23, Prov. 14:12). God's spokesmen are ever calling for men to "stand in the ways, and see, and ask for the old paths, where is the good way, and walk therein, and ye shall find rest for your souls" (Jeremiah 6:16).

FOREWORD

This little volume has come as a result of a series of studies presented by the author to a group of mature adults. When a search began to be made for a thoroughly documented source-book that might be used as a textbook, it was discovered there was none available. Although many good books and useful documents proved valuable in the research, there was nothing which fully documented the tenets of the religious groups under consideration. It is hoped that in this volume, both teachers and students who come after will find a reference book that will suffice in conducting a similar investigation anywhere and anytime.

If we know our heart, this undertaking has not been prompted by any motive other than a desire to see truth triumph over error, and to see God's name and way honored and glorified among men who love truth. We have not sought personal triumph in truth, but rather victory for God and His Word. He is convinced that opposition to the traditions of men should not be an occasion for one's vain display of personal talents or mental capacities, nor of his proficiency in logic nor ability to manipulate various passages of Scripture.

The truth of Christ requires no defense. Thus, we do not assail the position of another merely to defend our own. This is not necessary. The more frequently truth clashes with error, the brighter it will shine. The closer the two are brought side by side, the more apparent the difference becomes, and the more brilliant truth's lustre shall glow.

No Christian can maintain a neutral or passive attitude toward false ways. Through knowing God's Word he must conclude with David that he "hates every false way." He opposes error in a militant manner, as fervently as he embraces truth. His thinking must be both positive and negative.

Since the traditional errors originated by men are aggressively advocated by them and their followers, they will not die a natural death nor can we ignore them and expect them to go away. Error ceaselessly seeks to corrupt and neutralize the truth, and to destroy all whom it enmeshes in its tenacles. The great and final reason then for opposing error with truth is to deliver precious souls from its curses and to save them from bondage to freedom, from darkness to eternal light.

We have freely used quotations from many writers, to whom we gratefully acknowledge our indebtedness. We have done this deliberately, that the principal authorities and spokesmen of the various religious denominations might be allowed to "speak for themselves." No room has been left for doubting what they believe and teach.

Our aim has been always to "speak the truth in love," although we have realized that with the two-edged sword of the Spirit, we were piercing fiercely and fatally the untrue doctrines and commandments of men. We have not attacked men personally, for our wrestling is not against flesh and blood, but against the principles and powers of wickedness (Ephesians 6).

Thus we commit our efforts to their mission with the sincere prayer that God shall be honored, and that precious souls will be constrained to turn to the Lord and to "the faith once delivered unto the saints" (Jude 3).

Chapter One

ROMAN CATHOLICISM
[Part One]

BRIEF HISTORY. The first century church was established by Christ. It remained true as a whole, but even in early times some were departing from the faith (1Timothy 4:1-3). The form of church government was gradually changed by some men who desired preeminence in the churches. These men soon began to regard themselves as successors to the apostles. In 325 A.D., Constantine recognized the Council of Nicea as the first official church law-making assembly. He made Christianity the national religion of the Roman Empire and stopped all persecution against Christians. There were many changes in organization, worship, moral standards, name, etc., brought about by the various councils. In 608, Boniface proclaimed himself the "universal bishop" or "papa," setting the precedent for all subsequent popes, an office unknown prior to that time. The Council of 1870 (Vatican Council) proclaimed the doctrine of papal infalli-bility, culminating the authority claims for the traditions of the hierarchy, termed by Jesus as "doctrines and command-ments of men" (Matthew 15:7-9).

A major division occurred in 1054. The eastern division became known as the Greek Catholic Church ("The Holy Orthodox Catholic Apostolic Eastern Church"). The official name of the western church became "The Holy Catholic Apostolic and Roman Church."

I. Authority and the Bible

1. Tradition is to be held as the highest authority in the church, even above the Bible. "Other spiritual books ...are preferred" (Plain Facts For Fair Minds, Searle, p. 154).

1. Must not add to nor take from Scriptures inspired of God. Deuteronomy 4:2, Isaiah 8:20

2. Traditions of men make void the Word of God. Matthew 15:3, 6, 7-9. Worshipping thereby makes worship vain.

2. "If the sacred books are permitted everywhere. . .in the vernacular, there will arise...more harm than good" (Council of Trent, Schroeder, 273-8).

3. The Bible is not to be read by all; the Pope forbids it; all must not read it. (Catholic Dictionary, p. 82)

3. The Scriptures are alone sufficient for the man of God. 2 Timothy 3:15-17; Revelation 22:18-19; I Corinthians 4:6.

4. Scriptures are to be read and understood by everyone. Ephesians 3:4; John 5:39; Acts 17:11; I Peter 2:2; 2 Peter 1:20.

II. The Church

The Roman Catholic Church is the only true apostolic church.

"If it is not identical in belief, government, etc., with the primitive church, then it is not the Church of Christ." (Catholic Facts, p. 27)

1. No union of church and state in the Bible. Matthew 22:21; Romans 13:1-7.

2. Bible names for the church do not include "Roman" or "Catholic." Romans 16:16; I Corinthians

1:1; Hebrews 12:23; Acts 20:28.

3. Catholic church is described as the apostate church, the Mother of Harlots. Revelation 17:1-18.

  a. Rome on 7 hills. Revelation 17:9, 18.

  b. Rome on many waters, etc. Revelation 17:1, 15.

  c. Has the world drunk with spiritual fornication. Revelation 17:1-2

  d. Drunk with blood of martyrs. Revelation 17:6

  e. Mysterious. Revelation 17:5

  f. Called Babylon (confusion). Revelation 17:5

  g. Mother of Harlots (originator of all churches except Christ's).

III. Peter, Founder and Head of the Church

Peter established the church; he was the first pope and his successors were popes.

(Faith of our Fathers, p. 78).

"The records of the second century are so scanty as to throw but little light on the subject." Catholic Encyclopedia XII, p. 267.

1. Only the apostles could pass spiritual gifts to others. Acts 6:1-6; Acts 8:12-18; 19:6, 7; 2 Timothy 1:6.

2. Paul, an apostle, could pass spiritual gifts. Romans 1:10-11. The church at Rome evidently had never had an apostle visit them.

3. Peter denied the church was built by him or on him. I Peter 2:4-6.

4. Christ is the rock, "petra." I Corinthians 10:4. He is the builder and head

of the church. Matthew 16:18; Colossians 1:18; Ephesians 5:23

5. Peter was not superior to the other apostles. I Peter 5:1; 2 Corinthians 11:5; Acts 15:13-19; Matthew 20:25-26.

6. To be an apostle, one must have been a companion of Christ. Acts 1:21-22. Must have several qualifications which cannot be passed on by others.

7. Only one case of apostolic succession in Bible: Acts 1:15-26. When James was beheaded, no one was selected to succeed him like in the case of Judas. Acts 1:15-26; 15:1-29.

8. The only personal representative of Christ on earth is the Holy Spirit. John. 14:15-17, 26; 16:7, 13.

9. Peter was a married man. Matthew 8:14; I Corinthians 9:5. Popes are not allowed to marry.

10. Peter would not allow men to fall down to worship him. Acts 10:25, 26. See also Acts 14:14-15; Matthew 4:10. Not even an angel is to be worshipped by men. Revelation 19:10; 22:8-9.

IV. The Priesthood

1. The priest is 'another Christ,' the means of access between the sinner and God ..."who holds the place of God." (True Spouse of Christ, St. Ligouri, p. 93). "More certainty of doing the will of God by obedience to superiors than by obedience to Jesus Christ." (Ibid., p. 92-93)

1. Only one mediator--Christ 1 Timothy 2:5.
2. Christ has the only unchangeable high priesthood. Hebrews 7:11,12,22-24.
3. All Christians are priests who have access to God through Christ. 1 Peter 2:5-9; Revelation 1:5-6.

2. Catholics and non-Catholics are expected to call Priest "Father."

1. Call no man "Father" in religious sense. Matthew 23:9, 10.

3. Priest has power to forgive sins (Council of Trent, and Lateran Council of 1215). He receives gifts to say prayers. (Catholic Dictionary, Vatican Edition, p. 821.)

1. Forgiveness of sins belongs to the Godhead. Mark 2:6-10; 1 John 1:9; 2:1.
2. The gift of God cannot be purchased with money. 1 Peter 1:18.

V. Purgatory

There is an intermediate state or place called Purgatory where the dead go to suffer punishment until they can be purified. (Council of Florence, 1439) Made an official doctrine, though man began to teach the idea as early as the sixth century.

1. Prayers of saints or others cannot change our destiny after death. Hebrews 9:27.
2. The righteous acts of others cannot be transferred to my credit (before or) after my decease. I must answer for my own acts of my own body. 2 Corinthi-

These people have not fully made amends for their failings, so must atone for them by suffering before being admitted into heaven. These sufferings are lessened by prayers and masses, according to Council of Trent. (Fulton J. Sheen, World Book, "P", 803).

ans 5:10; Romans 2:6.

3. I cannot be saved by the prayers or righteous acts of others or even of my own self. Ephesians 2:8-9.

4. After death there is no changing from place of punishment to place of bliss. Luke 16:19-31.

5. The Bible knows nothing of indulgences either plenary or partial. Hebrews 2:3.

ROMAN CATHOLICISM
[Part Two]

VI. Concerning Morals
A. Killing

"The temporal sword is in the hand of Peter...spiritual and temporal...are in the power of the church...temporal authority is to be subjected to the spiritual." (Bull Unam Sanctum, November 18, 1302).

"The power of capital punishment is acknowledged for a perfect society...now the Catholic church is a perfect society." (Tablet, November 5, 1938):

"Holy" Wars justified by Church, called a "pious work," such as Crusades, "Full remission of sins," granted soldiers. (Disciplinary Decrees of the General Councils, Schroeder, 295).

1. "Thou shalt not kill." Exodus 20:13.
2. Murders forbidden. Romans 1:29.
3. Resistance and retaliation forbidden. Romans 12:19-21; Matthew 5:38-45. Love enemies and pray for them.

B. Adultery

Monks and nuns lived in same monastery since fourth century (Disciplinary Decrees of the General Coun-

1. "Thou shalt not commit adultery." Exodus 20:14. Principle is ageless.

15

cils, p. 154-155).

Permanent concubinage is not immoral (Catholic Encyclopedia, IV, p. 207).

Priest can forgive and absolve "an accomplice (partner in guilt) who is in danger of death" (New Code of Canon Law, p. 208).

Priest does not break vow of chastity by adultery (Explanation of Catholic Morals, p. 149). "All celibates are not chaste . . . one who takes the vow of celibacy does not break it by sinning against the sixth commandment; he is true to it till he weds."

C. Stealing

1. "Extreme necessity, when a person takes only what is necessary . . .
2. Secret compensation . . . when debtor cannot recover his property by any other means." (Manual of Christian Doctrine, p. 157, 297).

D. Lying

1. Doctrine of "mental reservation" permits Catholics to lie if by so doing they can further their religion. (Manual of Christian Doctrine, p. 444).

---

2. Lustful gaze as well as overt act sinful. Matthew 5:27-32; Galatians 5:19-21.

1. "Eye for eye" doctrine cancelled by Jesus as a ministration of death. 2 Corinthians 3:7-9; Matthew 5:38-39.

1. "Shalt not bear false witness." Exodus 20.
2. "Lie not one to another." Colossians 3:9.
3. "Speaking the truth in love." Ephesians 4:15.

"A Catholic who on being asked denies that he is one, does not necessarily deny the faith. Such answer might be a fitting reply to an impertinent question" (Manual of Moral Theology, I, p. 171-172).

"Do not live by fixed principles; live by opportunity and circumstances." (Handbook Oracle, Tarazona, Spain).

2. Relics are fakes: "Many of the more ancient relics duly exhibited for veneration . . . are either certainly spurious or open to grave suspicion." (Catholic Encyclopedia, XII, p. 737). Saint Christopher recently declared never to have existed!

4. Some will turn from truth. 2 Timothy 4:4.
5. Some receive not love for truth. 2 Thessalonians 2:10.
6. "Through hypocrisy that speak lies, branded in their conscience as with a hot iron." 1 Timothy 4:2.

VII. Baptism

1. Affusion, or sprinkling is sufficient for Baptism, as well as immersion: (Catholic Dictionary, Addis and Arnold, p. 60; Question Box, p. 366).

1. Baptism is a burial. Romans 6:4; Colossians 2:12.
2. Baptism is a planting. Romans 6:5.
3. Baptism is a resurrection. Colossians 2:12.
4. Baptism is a washing. Acts 22:16.
5. Baptism is a birth of water. John 3:5.
6. Baptism is a Greek word which is translated to "dip, plunge, submerge."

2. An infant should receive baptism. "Baptism, nowadays, is given almost exclusively to children." (Our Priesthood, Bruneau, p. 154).

3. He should be christened with the name of a "saint" and should have a "godfather and a godmother."

4. Original sin, inherited from Adam, is forgiven when the infant is baptized.

7. There is only one baptism. Ephesians 4:5.

8. Believers who have repented of their sins and confessed faith in Christ are Biblically qualified to be baptized. Romans 10:10; Acts 2:38; Mark 16:15-16.

9. All Christians are called saints. 1 Corinthians 1:2. Christening not in Bible, nor godfather or godmother.

10. Original sin not taught in Bible. No act or deed or guilt for such can be transmitted from one person to another. Ezekiel 18:20; 2 Samuel 12:23; Matthew 18:10; 19:14; Psalms 127:3-5. Children are innocent until they themselves sin by their own lust. James 1:13-15.

The child does not bear the guilt of his father or anyone else, though he may suffer the consequences of others' sins.

VIII. Confirmation

In Confirmation, the Holy Spirit is received by the hands of the bishop when the child reaches the age of accountability (about 12).

1. "Confirmation" ceremony is not taught in God's Word.

2. The Holy Spirit is given

(Catholic Dictionary, Addis and Arnold, p. 208).

when a believer is immersed. Acts 2:38; 5:32.

3. Only Christ prayed for Holy Spirit to be sent. John 14:15-17.

IX. Holy Eucharist

1. "Transubstantiation" is the change from bread and wine to the actual body and blood of Christ, performed at the consecration of the mass (adopted at the Lateran Council in 1215 A.D.)..

1. Christ was materially present when He gave the bread and fruit of the vine to the disciples and said, "This is my body," and "This is my blood." It is obviously a figure of speech (metaphor), the same as when He spoke of Himself as a "door" and as a "vine." John 10:7; 15.

He was not literally a vine or a door.

2. The communion (or "Eucharist") is an "unbloody" sacrifice of the mass.

2. There was only one offering of Christ; He was once sacrificed for our sins. Hebrews 6:6; 9:25-26; 10:11-12.

3. "Communion under one kind" allows "clergy" to receive the wine, and "laity" supposedly receive both body and blood in the one element, the bread.

3. Both bread and fruit of the vine are to be given to all Christians. Matthew 26:27; Mark 14:23; 1 Corinthians 11:28. There is no clergy—laity distinction among Christians in the Bible.

X. Extreme Unction

Health and strength to the soul and body at the point of death.

Must not go beyond what is written! 1 Corinthians 4:6. No such practice in Bible.

XI. Holy Orders & Dress

Holy Orders are said to be one of the seven sacraments by which the bishops, priests and officers of the church are ordained to office.

Peculiar attire (habits) distinguish each order.

1. Sacraments not in Bible.
2. Divisions, "Orders of Catholicism, are condemned in 1 Corinthians 1:10.

3. By fruits (not collars or robes) Jesus said we shall be known. Matthew 7:20.

XII. Matrimony

1. A "Sacrament whereby grace is imparted."
2. Marriage is void unless performed by a priest. All non-Catholics living in 'concubinage' instead of Christian matrimony (Question Box, p. 349,350) (Leo XIII, Life of Leo XIII, p. 332)
3. There is no cause for which the marriage bond may be broken.

4. No artificial birth control method may be employed in marriage, even if the life of the mother is in jeopardy.

(American Ecclesiastical Review, July 1948—quoted in Birth Control, by Alvin Jennings, Star Bible Publications, 1961, 24 pages.)

1. Bible silent. 2 John 9, 10, 11.
2. Where was the priest at the wedding Jesus attended? John 2:1-11. Marriage is not a "church ordinance" nor a "sacrament" according to the Bible.

3. Jesus allowed fornication as the sole cause for divorce. Matthew 5:32; 19:9.

4 1 Corinthians 3:17; Ephesians 5:29; 1 Peter 3:7—The Christian is to care for his body which is the temple of the Holy Spirit. Anything done deliberately which endangers health is sin.

XIII. Celibacy

"The law of celibacy of the clergy is not a divine institution but is a rule of the Church which developed gradually, and was finally made a part of the legal code for the greater part of the world" (Externals of the Catholic Church, Sullivan, p. 6).

1. Hebrews 13:4.
2. Bishop must be married. Titus 1:5-6; 1 Timothy 3:2.
3. Forbidding to marry a doctrine of devils. 1 Timothy 4:1-3.

XIV. Doctrine of Mary
(Glories of Mary—page numbers below)

1. Mary shunned the sight of men. 627, 641, 642.
2. She alone can obtain pardon. 51, 71, 83.
3. Cannot be saved without praying to Mary. 254, 255, 189.
4. Perpetual virgin; not defiled by man. 331.
5. Not subject to Christ. 200.
6. Mother of God. 202, 211.
7. "Assumption of Mary," doctrine defined in 1950.
8. "Immaculate Conception of Mary" doctrine originated in England; she was born without the stain of original sin. (Life of Blessed Virgin, De Gentilucci, 104-105).

1. Hebrews 13:4; 1 Corinthians 7:1-5.
2. Only one mediator, Jesus. 1 Timothy 2:5.
3. Colossians 3:17. All in the name of Christ.

4. Matthew 1:25. Joseph 'knew' her after Jesus' birth.
5. Christ Lord of all. Acts 10:36; Matthew 28:18-20.
6. Genesis 1:1.

Useful Books On Catholic Tradition

Catholicism Against Itself, Vol. 1 & 2, O.C. Lambert
Faith of Our Fathers, James Cardinal Gibbons (paper)
Churches of Today, Tomlinson (paper)
Confraternity New Testament (paper)
    or 4 version NT: RSV, KJ, Phillips, Catholic
Slides: Catholicism In the Light of the Bible

Note: All references quoted in chapters one and two are official publications of the Roman Catholic Church. Every volume quoted is on deposit at the library of Abilene Christian College through the generosity of the late O. C. Lambert.

Chapter Two

LUTHERANISM

Brief History:

The Lutheran Church is the oldest of existing Protestant churches. It can be traced to the Eve of All Saints Day, Oct. 31, 1517. On that date, Martin Luther (a Roman Catholic priest of the Sulpician order) nailed his 95 theses to the door of the Church at Wittenburg, Germany. He was principally opposing the sale of Indulgences as preached by Tetzel throughout Germany. Luther's intention was to reform the Roman Church, not to start a new one. However, ho: act started a great movement known as the Protestant Reformation.

Luther at the age of 20 obtained a complete copy of the Bible in a university library. He soon developed a great love and respect for it. He later entered a monastery, but when he saw the many evils in it, he quit and left it.

Various trials were held, and after Luther was given a chance to renounce his views but refused to do so, he was banned in 1521 from the Roman Church. He then started meeting on his own and soon had a sizeable following. The worship was similar to that of the Catholics.

(Schaff-Herzog, Vol. 2, p. 1363-72)

I. Creeds

Endorse Nicene Creed, Apostles Creed, Athanasian Creed and also the Augsburg Confession, and others (Luth Catechism, p. 81-82).

I. Creeds

1. John 6:63; Matthew 22:29.
2. 2 Timothy 3:16-17; 2 Peter 1:21.
3. Galatians 1:8-9; Matthew 10:20.

II. Different Church Branches.

The Lutheran Church is one of the branches along with other denominations. (L. Catechism, p. 108)
Evangelical L u t h e r a n church is the one established on Pentecost (L. Catechism, p. 110).

II. Different churches are not branches of Christ's Church.

1. Christ the head over the body. Ephesians 1:22-23.
2. One body, Ephesians 2:16; 4:4; I Corinthians 12:20
3. John 15:1-6. Man, not groups or denominations are spoken of. Abide in Christ.
4. How enter into Christ: Romans 6:3; Galatians 3:27.
5. Only planted one church. Matthew 15:13; 16:18.

III. Justified By Faith Alone

"Justification by f a i t h alone in Jesus Christ is held to be the central doctrine of the word of God" (Government Report of Denominations, Vol. 2, p. 853). Added "alone" to Romans 3:28, German Bible, See Catechism, p. 104.

III. Not justified by faith alone.

1. James 2:24. Not by faith alone.
2. James 2:19. Devils believe also.
3. John 12:42-3. Some who believed were not saved.
4. Matthew 10:32-33. Confession also necessary.
5. Gal. 5:6. Faith must work to avail.

LUTHERAN TRADITION	WORD OF GOD

IV. Baptized by Sprinkling or Pouring

Christ does not specify the mode of baptism. It may be performed in any one of three ways; namely, by sprinkling, pouring or immersion. One mode is just as valid as another.

(Luther's C a t e c h i s m. Stump, p. 147).

V. Baptize Infants

"Christ has commanded that little children should be brought to him and we obey this command by baptizing them and teaching them."

(Lutheran Catechism, Stump. p. 146).

"They (children) have inherited a sinful heart, and the germs of sin in them will soon grow"

(Lutheran Catechism, Stump, p. 146).

VI. Lord's Supper
A Sacrament through which forgiveness of sins is promised.

(Lutheran Catechism, p. 159).

'Always preceeded by ser-

IV. Baptize by sprinkling or pouring not right.

1. John 3:23. Much water.
2. Matthew 3:16. Up out of water after baptism.
3. Acts 8:38-39. Down into and up out of water.
4. Romans 6:4 Burial (Colossians 2:12)
5. Greek work is baptizo . . . to dip, plunge, submerge, Two other words for sprinkling and pouring.

V. Baptize Infants Unbiblical

1. Acts 17:29. We are offspring of God.
2. Mark 10:14. "Suffer the little children" . . .
3. Ezekiel 18:20. Son not guilty except for own sins.
4. No infant baptized.
5. Acts 8:12. Both men and women.
6. Mark 16:16. Belief comes first.

VI. Lord's Supper
1. Sacrament from Romanism, not Bible.
2. Forgiveness not through the partaking of the Lord's Supper.
3. Not in Bible.

LUTHERAN TRADITION	WORD OF GOD
vice of confession and absolution.' (Lutheran Catechism, p. 161).	
'Christ conferred upon the church the "Power of the Keys" to remit sins—so the minister uses the power and pronounces the absolution (Lutheran Catechism, p. 161).	4. Upon Apostles only. Matthew 16:18; 18:18.
The real presence of the bdoy and blood of Jesus are sacramentally and supernaturally received by those who partake of the communion." (Government Report, Vol. 2, p. 853).	5. A figure like John 10; and John 15. 6. Luke 22:19. Jesus was still in the flesh.
"With and Under"—consubstantiation doctrine is that "the bread and wine do not simply represent the body and blood of Christ (Zwingli's view)." (Lutheran Catechism, p. 156-7).	

VII. Observe Lent and Easter

Similar to Catholics, borrowed from them.

VII. No Lent nor Easter

1. Hebrews 1:2. God speaks through Christ only.
2. Hosea 2:11. Special days to cease.
3. Colossians 2:16-17. Not to be judged by special days.
4. Mark 16:9. The first day of the week is the only day

Christians distinguish from others.

5. Such days as Lent, Easter, Sabbath, Christmas, seasons, etc., not to be observed religiously.

VIII. Name Lutheran

Luther did not approve: "I pray you leave my name alone and not to call yourselves Lutherans but Christians. (Life of Luther, Michelet, p. 262).

VIII. Name Lutheran

1. Acts 4:12. No other name.
2. I Peter 4:16. Name Christian.
3. Acts 26:28. Name Christian.
4. Acts 11:26. Name Christian.

IX. The Ten Commandments

The Ten Commandments are for us and all God's creatures. (Lutheran Catechism, p 41-42).

(They omit the 2nd Commandment in their listing, like Catholics do). Lutheran Catechism, p. 17.

IX. Ten Commandments

1. II Corinthians 3:7-11. Passed away.
2. Colossians 2:14-17. Nailed to cross.
3. Galatians 5:1-4. Severed from Christ if justified by law.
4. Romans 7:1-4. Discharged from law.

X. The Christian Sabbath

Lutherans teach Sunday is the Christian Sabbath, the Lord's Day.

X. The Christian Sabbath

1. Sabbath is the 7th day of week. Exodus 20:8-11.
2. Lord's Day is the first day of the week. Matthew 28:1-10; John 20:19-29; Acts 20:7; 1 Corinthians 16:1-2; Revelation 1:10.

LUTHERAN TRADITION	WORD OF GOD

XI. Baptism and Circumcision

Circumcision was received by children as a token of the covenant—"so now children are to be baptized and receive the token of the new covenant, the seal of the righteousness of faith."

(Luther's Small Catechism under Question, 335.)

"...circumcision, which is a type of baptism."

(Lutheran Catechism, Stump, p. 146).

Martin Luther

XI. Baptism & Circumcision

1. Circumcision of flesh was a shadow of circumcision of the heart. Hebrews 10:1; Romans 2:29.
2. Baptism never compared to circumcision in Bible; if so, then why female children baptized? Only males were circumcized.

Chapter Three

PRESBYTERIANISM

Brief History:

Among the earliest of the 'Protestant Reformers' was John Calvin (1509-1564). He was born in Noyon, France to Roman Catholic parents. Calvin was converted from Romanism in 1533, and during the following three years he lived in seclusion under an assumed name.[1] He studied the New Testament in the original language, and though he did not start a distinct sect in his day, he was founder of the doctrine that wears his name, Calvinism. It is usually associated with Presbyterianism, although a number of churches which are not Presbyterian in government hold to Calvin's tenets.

The word Presbyterian comes from the Greek word presbuteros (elder); hence, a Presbyterian church is governed by elders. The doctrine and church government system was transferred to Scotland from France, Holland and Geneva. There, under the leadership of John Knox, Presbyterianism became very strong. The Church of Scotland came into existence and the first book of discipline was written in 1560;

---

1. Lingle, W.A. Presbyterianism: Their History and Beliefs. 1944. p. 25-26.

1592 marked the acceptance by Parliament of Presbyterianism as the established state church.[2]

The Westminster Association, in session from 1643-1649, framed the Westminster Confession of Faith. This became the doctrinal standard for both English and American Presbyterianism. Francis Makemie is considered the founder of American Presbyterianism, for he organized the Rehoboth Presbyterian Church in Maryland in 1684. There have been seventeen distinct segments of Presbyterians from near the beginning of the movement.

Calvin followed a simple worship in his churches. There was congregational singing, a departure from his early experience in the Roman Catholic Church. They used no instruments of music, for Calvin opposed such as a departure from New Testament worship, borrowed from Romanism. He broke away from the altar worship pattern, and placed the reading and preaching in the central place. Strict moral discipline was exercised (for cursing, adultery, playing cards on Sunday evenings, spending time in taverns, betrothing a Papist, wife beating, etc.)

The five points of Calvinism are: Total Depravity, Unconditional Election, Limited Atonement, Irresistable Grace, and Preserverence of the Saints. James Arminius, a professor at the University of Leyden, opposed the other professors for their 'high Calvinism' in a theological battle that lasted several years.[3]

---

2. Schaff-Herzog Encyclopedia, Vol. III, p. 1892.
3. Lingle, op. cit., p. 29-42.

1. "God has predestined and foreordained some men and angels out of his free grace and love without any foresight of faith in either of them, and others are foreordained to everlasting death and the number of either is so certain and definite that it cannot be increased or diminished."
-Westminster Confession of Faith, Article 3, 4, 5; Chapter 3; Article 2, Chapter 10.

1. Salvation is for all who believe and obey the gospel. John 3:16; Hebrews 5:9; Matthew 28:18-20; Mark16: 15-16; Romans 10:9-17; 6: 1-18; Acts 2:38,39; 2 Thessalonians 2:14; 1:7-8; 2 Peter 1:10.
2. God is no respector of persons. Acts 10:34; 2 Peter 3:9; I Timothy 2:3-4; 1 John 4:14.

2. God's Grace is so irresistable, that one cannot help yielding to it if he is among the elect; he has no choice, but must be saved.
(Doctrine of Irresistable Grace)

1. Man must choose for himself whom he will serve, Jehovah God or false gods. Joshua 24:15.
2. I Kings 18:21. Elijah called for a decision between the two sides.
3. Obedience is from our own mind and heart. Romans 6:17-18.

3. God's Atonement was sufficient for all, but efficient only for the elect.
(See Lingle, p. 41).

1. II Corinthians 12:9. Grace is sufficient.
2. II Corinthians 9:8. All sufficiency in all things.
3. Romans 5:6. Christ died for the ungodly.
4. II Corinthians 5:14. "One died for all . . ."

PRESBYTERIAN TRADITION	WORD OF GOD
4. One cannot fall from God's grace; it is an utter impossibility. (Calvin's doctrine of Perserverance of Saints)	1. Judas did fall. Acts 1:25. 2. You may fall. Hebrews 12:15; I Corinthians 10:12. 3. Some did fall. Galatians 5:4. 4. Paul feared he might fall I Corinthians 9:27. 5. Some will be taken out of the kingdom, the group of saved ones. Acts 2:47; John 3:3-5; Matthew 13:41. 6. We labor in hope of eternal life. Titus 1:2.
5. There are three baptismal modes; immersion is not necessary, but one may be sprinkled or poured. (Presbyterian Confession of Faith, Chapter 30, p. 157).	1. Buried. Romans 6:3-4. Colossians 2:12. 2. Washed. Hebrews 10:22; Titus 3:5; 3. One baptism. Ephesians 4:5. 4. Birth. John 3:5. 5. Going down into, coming up out of. Acts 8:36-9.
6. Infants of one or both believing parents are to be baptized. (Presbyterian Confession of Faith, Chapter 30, p. 157). Voted by Westminster Assembly, 1643-9. Carried: 25 to drop dipping and 24 to retain sprinkling.	1. Acts 8:12. Men and women. 2. Mark 16:16. Belief precedes. 3. Acts 2:38. Repentance precedes. 4. John 6:45. Must hear and learn before coming to Jesus.
7. Faith alone will save a person.	1. James 2:14, 17, 19, 22, 24, 26. 2. John 1:12. "Power to

become" sons of God if believe.
3. John 12:42. Some be-
lieved, yet lost.

8. Confession of the Apostles' Creed is necessary.

1. Matthew 16:16. Christ
is our only "Creed".
2. Matthew 16:18. Christ
built his church upon the
confession of that truth.
3. The only confession: Acts
8:38-39; Romans 10:10;
Matthew 10:32-33; I John 4:
2.

9. Communion is not to be
observed weekly.
"And truly this custom,
which enjoins communing
once a year is most wicked
contrivance of the devil, by
whose instrumentality so-
ever it may have been determined."
Calvin's Institutes, Book 4,
Chapter 17.
"It ought to have been
far otherwise. Every week at
least the table of the Lord
should have been spread for
Christian assemblies."
Calvin's Institutes, Book 6,
Chapter 18.

1. Leviticus 24:5-9. Shew-
bread weekly, shadow (Hebrews 10:1) of new.
2. Acts 2:42. Steadfastly.
3. Acts 20:7. Early church
communed weekly.

10. The Holy Spirit acts
directly upon the heart of
the elect to persuade him to
obey the call of the Gospel.

1. Christ prayed for Holy
Spirit to come to apostles.
John 14:15-17.

33

"We believe in the Holy Spirit, the Lord and Giver of Life, who moves everywhere upon the heart of men to restrain them from evil and to incite them to good . . . and to persuade them to obey the call of the Gospel." -General Assembly in Los Angeles, 1903.

2. Promised to those who repent and are baptized. Acts 2:38; 5:32.

3. Holy Spirit assisted preachers directly in New Testament, but never operated directly on sinner in saving him. Acts 8:26-39.

John Calvin

Chapter Four

EPISCOPALIANISM

Brief History:

An Episcopalian is a member of the Protestant Episcopal Church—one branch of the Anglican Church or Church of England. Today there are forty million Anglicans throughout the world. They all use the Common Book of Prayer. This religious group has been called the "bridge church" between Roman Catholic and Protestant. It preserves the Catholic sacraments and creeds, but rejects the authority of the Bishop of Rome (the Pope).[1]

The Episcopal Church had its beginning from 1531-1539 when Henry VIII, King of England, resorted to political necessity in order to accomplish and justify his divorce from Catherine, and his subsequent marriage to Ann Boleyn. He had passed the "Act of Supremacy" which made him "the only supreme head in earth of the Church of England." Thus was severed the tie with papal communion, and was established an independent body in England. Henry soon abolished

---

1. Rosten, Leo. Religions of America. Article: What Is An Episcopalian? by Norman Pettinger, p. 48-49.

monastic establishments and confiscated their wealth (amounting to 38,000,000 pounds). It was common knowledge that his break with Rome was not prompted by doctrinal reform or differences.[2]   Henry VIII in this way became for all practical purposes the "Pope of England." The Thirty Nine Articles of Faith and their Prayer Book govern the church.

Episcopalian clergymen deny that Henry VIII founded the Episcopalian Church. They simply affirm that it was during his time that "freedom of the English Church from the authority of the Bishop of Rome was achieved," and that then was ended a long period of protest and agitation against the Roman pope's usurpations of authority.[3]

The ecclesiastical connections between the Church of England and the English colonists in the new world were broken during the War of Revolution and the Church of England in the colonies became known as the Protestant Episcopal Church in the United States. The word 'Episcopal' comes from the Greek 'episcopos,' meaning overseer.

Henry VIII

2. Schaff-Herzog Encyclopedia. Vol. I, p. 726.
3. Rosten, op. cit.

EPISCOPALIAN TRADITION	WORD OF GOD
1. The church should be governed by one bishop who rules over a diocese of several local churches.	1. In the Bible, never was one bishop or overseer over several churches. The "Diocesan Episcopacy" was unknown. 2. Elder and bishop are two names for the same office in the New Testament. Acts 20:17,28; Titus 1:5-7; I Peter 5:1-3. 3. A plurality of elders (also called bishops, overseers, presbyters, shepherds, pastors) guided the local body of believers; there is no case of one man over one church or one man over a plurality of churches. See Acts 14:23; 15:2,22,23; 16:4; Philippians 1:1-2; I Timothy 3:1-7; 5:17.
2. The twelve "great facts of the Apostles' Creed" are to be obeyed. (J. P. Norris, Catechism and Prayer Book, p. 9).	1. The Bible and the Bible only is the Christian's rule of faith and practice. 2 John 9-11; II Timothy 3:16-17. 2. The 'Apostle's Creed', so-called, was not written by the apostles.
3. What the parents promise for the child at his or her baptism, the child is bound to believe and obey. (Norris, Ibid., p. 18).	1. Every person is accountable for his own choices and his own deeds. (See arguments under Presbyterianism where Calvinism is discussed.)

2. No Bible passage authorizes a father or mother to make promises for what a child shall believe or obey. Beware of doctrines and commandments of men that make void the word of God! Matthew 15:7-9; Mark 7:6-7.

4. A person must obey the Ten Commandments as recorded in Exodus chapter 20, because his parents bound it upon him at baptism . . . as well as the "Apostles' Creed." (Norris, Ibid.).

1. A person who endeavors to be justified by the law given by Moses is "severed from Christ" and "fallen away from grace," Galatians 5:4; 2 Corinthians 3:7-11; Galatians 3:24-25.
2. The law was taken away, changed. Colossians 2:14-17; Hebrews 7:12; 10:1-4.

5. Christ taught us the "Lord's Prayer" and we should pray it today, including "Thy Kingdom come," because the kingdom only came "imperfectly" on the Day of Pentecost . . . it is a prayer for church extension and for Second-Advent. (Norris, p. 34-41).

1. Disciples were never instructed after the Day of Pentecost to petition God that the kingdom might come in any sense whatsoever. The kingdom "came with power" on that Day; nothing failed that God designed for it. Isaiah 2:2-4; Mark 9:1; Acts 1:8; 2:1-47.

6. "Forms of prayers" are recommended by the Lord. (Norris, p. 42).

1. Our prayers are not to be stereotyped, lip-service, such as is characterized by memorized prayers. Matthew 6: 1, 5-15; Mark 7:5-13.
2. The Lord's Prayer is recorded in John chapter 17.

EPISCOPALIAN TRADITION   WORD OF GOD

Obviously he did not intend that any prayer be a repetition of mechanical memorized utterances of the lips.

7. After the Hampton Court Conference (1604), two sacraments are held to be "necessary to salvation"—Baptism and the Supper of the Lord.
(Ibid., p. 48ff).
"Sacrament is an outward and visible sign of an inward and spiritual grace given unto us." Baptism makes infants children of God, members of Christ; imparts remission of sins.
(Ibid., p. 50-51, and Book of Common Prayer, p. 230).

1. Sacraments is a word not in the Bible, but let us here consider Baptism as administered by them is sprinkling or pouring water upon an infant for his salvation.
2. Much water required. John 3:23.
3. Went into water. Acts 8:38.
4. Were buried in water. Colossians 2:12; Romans 6:3-4.
5. Came up out of water. Acts 8:39. (Never was water brought to a person for baptism in the early church times.
6. If water is all a person receives in baptism for his salvation, then this is water salvation. This is all a baby receives for it is too young to be taught, to believe, to repent, to confess.
7. Faith and repentance are pre-requisites for all candidates of baptism. Mark 16:16; Acts 2:38.

8. Infants are born in sin, in a state of sin, inherited from their parents . . . "being by

1. Infants do not sin. Romans 4:15.
2. Sin is transgression of law.

39

nature born in sin and the children of wrath."
(Ibid., p. 51, 62).

3. Sin is always an act of the mind or body, hence cannot be transferred to or inherited by another. James 1:14-15.

4. Children do not bear the guilt of their parents' sin. Ezekiel 18:17 — and also chapter 33.

5. Children are a gift from God. Matthew 18:3; Mark 10:14.

6. Of such is the kingdom of God. Matthew 18:3, 10 Mark 10:14.

7. People go astray; are not born astray. Psalms 14:3; Isaiah 59:2.

8. We are the offspring of God. Acts 17:29.

9. God is the Father of our Spirits. Hebrews. 12:9.

9. "Immersion is the rule of the church, and baptism by affusion (pouring water over the child's head) is the exception . . . but practically affusion has become adopted and immersion seldom desired."
(Ibid., p. 223).

1. There is one baptism. Ephesians 4:5.

2. Baptism is a burial in water. (see above)

3. Traditions of men are self-condemned and those who worship thereby are doing so in vain, said our Lord (Matthew 15:1-9).

10. "Confirmation is the connecting link between the sacraments. It looks backward to Baptism, and forward to Holy Communion . . . possibly from the first

1. Those whose faith was confirmed were already Christians, having been previously baptized as adults. Acts 14:22; 15:41; 8:5-20.

2. It was never a "service"

called 'Communion'!"
(Ibid., p. 233).

Evangelists could baptize but only apostles could confirm, and the Holy Spirit was given at confirmation, not at baptism.
(Ibid., p. 234-5).

Candidates for Confirmation are required to acknowledge, renew and ratify their baptism obligations made by their parents for them when in infancy.
(Ibid., p. 237-255).

or ceremony for children at a set age who had come to an age of responsibility or accountability. The unwarranted practice of infant baptism left a void in the person's life ordinarily filled by baptism of his own choosing and as a result of his own instruction and faith at a time when he reached an age of accountability.

3. The Holy Spirit is given to all those who obey Christ from their own heart, at baptism. Acts 2:38; 5:32; Romans 6:3-4; 17-18.

4. When disciples were confirmed in the early church it was simply a strengthening, encouraging, etc.; it was never accompanied by a "first communion", obviously a purely human arrangement "after the precepts of men." Those who so practice truly make void God's truth regarding true baptism to which every accountable person should and would have access, were it not for the "doctrines and commandments of men."

11. Christ died to reconcile God to man. (Article 2, Prayer Book).

1. The opposite is true: Christ came to reconcile us to the Father. We were in need of being brought back, II Corinthians 5:18-19; Romans 5:10.

Chapter Five

METHODISM

Brief History:

Although John Wesley lived and died in the Episcopal Church, he founded the large and popular denomination known as the Methodist Church. In 1729, he and his brother, Charles, and a number of others began meeting for religious exercises. These people were students at Oxford University. These "Holy Clubs" wanted to overcome the formalism and ritualism of the Episcopal Church, and to stimulate piety and spirituality among its members. They arranged a daily schedule of duties, setting hours for visiting the sick and in prison, praying aloud three times each day, etc., etc.

The "turning point" in John Wesley's life came May 24, 1738 when at a prayer meeting in London, he learned that it is not by rules and laws nor by our own efforts at self-perfection, but by faith that man enters "upon life and peace."[1]

As other groups began to meet, they became known as Methodists because of their methodical manner of life. When Wesley died, the groups banded together under a conference known as the Methodist Episcopal Church. The bands at first

---

1. Harmon, N. B. (Editor). Doctrines and Discipline of The Methodist Church. Nashville: The Methodist Publishing House, 1948, p. 3.

were known simply as "Societies" following the General Rules drawn up by Wesley.

In 1784, Wesley took a step that formally put him out of the Church of England. When he was called upon to send ministers to America, he asked the Bishop of London to ordain several of his lay-preachers. The Bishop refused, so Wesley took the matter into his own hands and ordained two himself to preside over affairs in America including a Dr. Coke . . . whom he named Superintendent. Wesley died in 1791.[2]

The Methodist Episcopal Church of the United States had its beginning when the Christian Conference convened in Baltimore on December 24, 1784. At this conference, the Book of Discipline prepared by Wesley was adopted which cut the 39 Articles of the Episcopal Church down to 24 Articles, then added one to cover the church rulers in the United States. The Apostles' Creed (inherited by the Episcopal Church from the Catholic Church) was also brought into the Methodist form of worship.

Two notable divisions occurred. In 1828, a group separated becoming known as the Methodist Protestant Church. In 1844 there was another division having to do with slavery and with the powers of the General Conference. In 1939, three main divisions united to form the Methodist Church: (1) The Methodist Episcopal Church, (2) The Methodist Episcopal Church, South, and (3) The Methodist Protestant Church.

There are over nine million Methodists in the United States, besides 845,000 "preparatory members." Worldwide, Methodists claim 25 million membership.[3]

2. Schaff-Herzog Encyclopedia, Vol. II, p. 1485-6.
3. Harmon, op. cit.

METHODIST TRADITION	WORD OF GOD
1. "The Methodist Church is a church of Christ in which 'the pure word of God is preached and the Sacraments duly administered." Harmon, p. 3. Doctrines and Discipline of the Methodist Church.	1. The name "Methodist" not in the Bible. 2. The name "churches of Christ" is in the Bible. Romans 16:16. 3. "Sacraments" not in Bible, but even if it were, the Methodist church does not "duly administer" them according to the Bible. See under Baptism below for example.
2. Some Methodists do not believe in the virgin birth of Jesus Christ, and the church accepts them in this unbelief. R. Sockman, "What is A Methodist?", p. 82, article in Religions of America.	1. Jesus Christ was born of a virgin. Isaiah 7:14. Matthew 1:25. 2. Those who believe a lie are condemned. 2 Thessalonians 2:11-12.
3. There are two Sacraments, Baptism and the Lord's Supper. Sockman, Ibid. p. 86.	1. "Sacrament" is a word carried over from Catholic tradition, not found in the Scriptures.
4. "Let every adult person, and the parents of every child to be baptized, have the choice of sprinkling, pouring, or immersion." Discipline, p. 410.	1. Baptism was immersion or "burial" in and "raising up" from water. Romans 6:3-4; Colossians 2:12. 2. There was and is only one baptism. Ephesians 4:5.
5. "The baptism of Infants" is justified on basis Jesus said "Suffer the children to come unto me." Discipline, article, 1910, p. 470-4.	1. Baptism is not the subject Jesus was teaching on this occasion . . . not mentioned in this entire chapter, nor in the chapter before or after.

METHODIST TRADITION	WORD OF GOD
	2. Infants were never baptized in all Bible history.
6. Parents of the infant are duty bound to teach the infant after baptism, concerning "our faith" (Methodist Doctrine). Discipline, p. 471.	1. Teaching <u>preceded</u> true baptism, Matthew 28:18-20, as well as followed it. Infants are not capable of instruction, hence never received baptism in the Biblical record.
7. The Methodist Discipline gives rules, doctrines, and regulations governing all procedures and affairs of the church, and all ministers are obligated to observe "every part" of it in his district. Discipline, article 362, p. 108.	1. The Scriptures constitute God's only authorized guide, given by inspiration of God. 2 Timothy 3:16-17. 2. "All things pertaining unto life and godliness" were delivered in the first century. 2 Peter 1:3. 3. No other doctrine, principle, precept, commandment, procedure or policy is to be taught by man or angel, other than that given to the apostles. Galatians 1:8-9. 4. Nothing can be added to or taken from the word of God. Revelation 22:18-19. 5. Traditions or doctrine (disciplines) of men make void the word of God.
8. The complex organization of the Methodist Church with all its conferences, powers and duties are set forth in the Discipline. Discipline, article 4, p. 10.	1. The church of Christ had no ecclesiastical governing conferences. 2. Each local congregation was independent of all others, under Christ alone as head with all authority. Co-

lossians 1:18; Ephesians 1: 22-23.

3. Elders and deacons constituted local officers. Philippians 1:1; Titus 1:5; 1 Timothy 3:1-13.

9. Conferences must not change or revoke any of the Methodist Church's existing Articles of Religion, or change or do away with the episcopacy or destroy the superintendency.

1. Any Christian or group of Christians must repent of any man-made tradition, system or notion contrary to God's Word, and pray that God will forgive him of same. Acts 8:14-24.

2. Every man in any false way should renounce it, confess faith in Jesus Christ as the Son of God, and be immersed into the Kingdom of God, like Saul of Tarsus did. Acts 9; Acts 22.

3. "Come ye out from among them, and be ye separate." 2 Corinthians 6:17.

10. No member of the Methodist Church may preach without a license.

Discipline, article 302, p. 91.

1. Every Christian preached. Acts 8:4.

11. Women may engage in the ministry of preaching except as travelling evangelists.

Discipline, Article, 313, p. 94.

1. Not permitted. 1 Corinthians 14:34; 1 Timothy 2: 12.

METHODIST TRADITION	WORD OF GOD
12. Elders and deacons are selected by the election of the annual conference. Discipline, article 392, p. 115.	1. The local church is to select its officers from among themselves. Acts 6: 3-5. 2. Let them be proved, let them be chosen and then let them serve. 1 Timothy 3:1-10. 3. Evangelists appointed elders. Titus 1:5.
13. Term "Reverend" is applied to Methodist men. Discipline, article 414, p. 119	1. 'Reverend' used once in the Bible and there it applies to God, not man. Psalms 111: 9
14. The Methodist Publishing House shall be under the control of the Board of Publication, subject to the Conference. Discipline, article 1103, p. 238.	1. No conferences nor official functionaries of such in the early church. 1 Corinthians 4:6. Must not go beyond things written.
15. The order for dedication of an organ is prescribed: "in the name of the Father, Son and Holy Spirit." Discipline, article 1931, p. 550.	1. No organs in Christian's worship. Not according to the pattern. Hebrews 8:5. John Wesley objected to their use, as did all prominent reformers. 2. Cannot be "in name of Father, Son, and Holy Spirit."
16. The doctrine of "justification of faith only is a most wholesome doctrine and very full of comfort." Discipline, article 9.	1. See James 2:14-26. 2. Faith only gives us "power to become" sons of God. John 1:12. "Power to become suggests possibility,

not actuality.

3. Faith must work by love to avail with God. Galatians 5:6.

METHODIST TRADITION	WORD OF GOD
17. Immersion (baptism) is not essential for salvation of adults (although they do hold infants are saved by baptism!).	1. Baptism is necessary to: a. enter Kingdom. John 3:5. b. have sins forgiven. Acts 2:38. c. receive Holy Spirit. Acts 2:38. d. enter the church. 1 Corinthians 12:13. e. enter into Christ. Galations 3:27. f. save us. 1 Peter 3:21. g. wash away sins. Acts 22:16. h. save us. Mark 16:16.
18. It is not necessary to partake of Lord's Supper weekly; quarterly is practice of Methodists.	1. See type in Old Testament of weekly eating showbread. 1 Peter 2:5, 9; Revelation 1: 6; Leviticus 24:5-9; Hebrews 10:1. 2. Early Christians communed each week. Acts 20: 7; see 1 Corinthians 16:1-2. 3. Steadfastly. Acts 2:42.
19. The church is composed of many branches (denominations) and the Methodist church is one branch. Preamble to Constitution.	1. Christ established one church. Matthew 16:18; Acts 20:28; Romans 12:4-5; 1 Corinthians 10:17; Colossians 1:18; 1 Corinthians 12:13.

2. No division exists. 1 Corinthians 1:10.

3. If many denominations are the visible branches where is the visible trunk?

4. Jesus taught that "a man" is the branch and that Christ himself is the vine. John 15:1-7.

John Wesley

Chapter Six

BAPTIST

Brief History:

The first known Baptist church was organized in 1607 by John Smyth in London (David Benedict, History of Baptists, p. 304). The early history of Baptists is obscure, and adherents to that denomination are divided among themselves concerning their history. Some contend Smyth re-baptized himself by pouring water on himself; others contend he was baptized by John Morton in 1606 in the Don River at midnight (Schaff-Herzog Encyclopedia, Vol. III, p. 2202). The group started in America when Ezekiel Holliman baptized Roger Williams; Williams then baptized Holliman and several others (Ibid., p. 2531-2) at Providence, Rhode Island. The Baptist Encyclopedia says this occurred in March, 1639, thus marking the date of the oldest Baptist church in America (Vol. II, p. 1252. V. C. Vedder in his Short History of the Baptists, p. 291, gives practically the same account, except he records that Ezekiel Holliman had formerly been a member of his church at Salem before he baptized Williams in 1639.)

The name Baptist was not at first adopted by them. They preferred to be known as Brethren, Disciples of Christ, Christians or Believers (A. H. Newman, History of the Baptist churches in the United States, p. 1). The name Baptist was first claimed in 1644, and these people have worn it ever since (W. H. Whelsitt, A Question In Baptist History, p. 93).

51

Generally, Baptists today (there are some 28 different bodies among them in the United States alone) have no confession of faith and are congregational in their form of government. In their earlier history they did follow human creeds and they required each congregation to subscribe to them. One was written in London in 1677 and was adopted by the Particular Baptists in 1689. It was later accepted by the American Baptists in Philadelphia in 1742, known from that date as the Philadelphia Confession of Faith. J. Newton Brown of New Hampshire wrote a confession in 1833 which was adopted by the New Hampshire Conference; it became known as the New Hampshire Confession of Faith. While the Philadelphia Confession is strongly Calvinistic, the New Hampshire document is only "mildly" Calvinistic—it is the most popular confession among Baptists. (See W. J. McGlothlin's Baptist Confessions of Faith, p. 299; also Hiscox, The Standard Manual For Baptist Churches, p. 56.)

Although the Baptists do not conform to their manual like the Methodists do to their Discipline, it is nevertheless an accurate statement of their beliefs. Primitive Baptists, Missionary Baptists and then Free Will Baptists were the first to appear in America, of course followed by various other branches. By 1966, their 28 bodies in America had 92,000 churches with 21,500,000 members. Most Baptists in this country belong to one of four major groups: The American Baptist Convention, The National Baptist Convention of America, the National Baptist Convention U.S.A., Inc., and the Southern Baptist Convention. Baptists throughout the world belong to the Baptist World Alliance (W. H. Porter, "Baptists," World Book Encyclopedia, 1966).

BAPTIST TRADITION	WORD OF GOD

1. Creeds

Members who are received into fellowship "are not required to subscribe or pledge conformity to any creed-form, but are expected to yield substantial agreement to that which the church with which they unite has adopted." (Hiscox, Standard Manual of Baptist Churches, p. 56, American Baptist Association.)

The Bible is the supreme standard for all creeds, etc. (Hiscox, p. 58).

1. Scriptures alone tell man how to behave in the house of God, the church. 1 Timothy 3:14-17.

2. Why should the "church" adopt or subscribe to a man-made creed and its members "be expected" to agree substantially thereto? Matthew 15:7-9; Revelation 22:18-19.

2. Divine Election, Predestination

(American) Baptists are decidedly Calvinistic. A person is dead in sin and cannot do one thing to rescue himself. If one is saved, it is because God elected to save him before the foundation of the world.
(Standard Manual, Hiscox, p. 57).

1. 2 Peter 3:9: God does not will that any perish.

2. 1 Timothy 2:3, 4: God would have all saved.

3. Hebrews 5:9: Christ saves all who obey.

4. Colossians 3:25: God no respector of persons.

5. Ephesians 1:3-7: God ordained that all who are saved shall be saved in Christ. Not that He picked individuals and omitted individuals before the world began.

3. Eternal Security

"We believe that such only are real believers as endure to the end."
(Church Manual Designed For Use of Baptist Churches, J. M. Pendleton, p. 54).

1. Acts 8:13: Simon believed and was baptized and continued for a time.

2. Hebrews 10:26: some sin willfully.

3. Hebrews 6:1-6: Once

BAPTIST TRADITION	WORD OF GOD
[Free Will Baptists do not believe this.] "Such as are truly regenerate will not utterly fall away." (Hiscox, *op. cit.*, p. 67).	saved, some later were lost. 4. Galatians 5:4: Some did fall from grace. 5. 1 Corinthians 9:27: Paul saw danger of falling and being rejected. 6. 21 books of New Testament written to Christians, much of which is warnings of danger of being lost. 7. Luke 8:13: Some believe, then fall away. 8. John 3:3-5: None in the Kingdom except the regenerated, but some of these will be cast out of Kingdom into lake of fire. Matthew 13:41, 42, 43. 9. John 8:31: IF ye continue . . .
4. The church was established during the days of John the Baptist. (Landmarkism: What Is It?, p. 121). [Some say it was at the calling of the 12; others only affirm it was sometime during the personal ministry of Christ.]	1. Matthew 16:18: I <u>will</u> build; nothing prevail against establishing it. 2. Church spoken of as in existence after Acts 2, the day of Pentecost. 3. Kingdom came with power, Acts 1:8; Mark 9:1, Acts 2:1-4, when Holy Spirit came. 4. John was already dead. Matthew 14:10-12; 11:11.
5. Faith Alone Saves ". . . solely through faith."	1. James 2:17: Faith without works is dead. 2. James 2:18: Faith shown by works.

BAPTIST TRADITION	WORD OF GOD
(Hiscox, op. cit., p. 62. This is contradicted on p. 61: "wholly of grace"???)	3. James 2:19: Faith alone characterizes devils. 4. James 2:24, 26: Faith only not enough. 5. Galatians 5:6: Faith working through love. 6. Mark 16:16: Faith plus baptism equals salvation. 7. See Hebrews 11: Faith in action avails.
6. Confession at Baptism The baptismal candidate is asked to confess that he believes God has pardoned his sins, even before baptism (a common practice).	1. Matthew 16:16: This is correct confession. 2. Acts 8:37: This is the correct confession. 3. Matthew 10:32: Confess Christ. 4. Acts 2:38: Baptism is "for remission of sins"; thus Baptists ask candidates to confess an untruth.
7. Baptism is an immersion, but "NOT essential to salvation." (Hiscox, p. 20, Note 8). Must be baptized in order to enter the Baptist church; baptism is a "church ordinance." (Pendleton, p. 65, 90). Must relate 'experience' then the membership votes whether to receive new member and allow him to be baptized. (Pendleton, p. 17, 103; Hiscox, p. 23).	1. Mark 16:16: baptism preceeds salvation. 2. Acts 2:38: for remission of sins. 3. John 3:5: birth of water and spirit essential to entering Kingdom of heaven. 4. Galatians 3:27: to enter Christ (saved without Christ?) 5. 1 Peter 3:21: baptism saves. 6. Acts 22:16: sins washed away at baptism. 7. Romans 6:3-4: baptized into Christ's death and into

Early church quickly received new member. Now it is different! Must now vote! Read entire page 22, Hiscox. [NOTE: "There is a maxim of law, that the expression of one thing is the exclusion of another. It must be so; for otherwise there could be no definiteness in contracts . . . illustrated 1000 ways. . . God commanded Noah to build an ark out of gopher wood . . . forbids the use of every other kind of wood." (Pendleton, p. 81).

his body, the church. 1 Corinthians 12:20.

8. Galatians 3:26-27 and 1 Corinthians 12:20: Baptism ushers one (1) into Christ and at the same time (2) into his body, the church. The saved are thus added to the church. Acts 2:47. [It is harder to enter the Baptist Church than to enter heaven, according to Baptist tradition.]

9. Acts 8:26-39: No church vote or ordinance here. God commands baptism for salvation. Any man can obey without delay or probation.

10. 2 John 9-11: No change is permitted in practice, precept, or policy. Who changed and made it different? Man and his traditions which make void the word of God.

This principle if applied would prohibit all the traditions of the Baptist Church: the name Baptist Church, voting on new members, the unscriptural confession, use of instrumental music in worship, etc., etc.

8. Use instruments of Music In Worship

Not in Christian worship as revealed in New Testament. Leading Baptists have

BAPTIST TRADITION	WORD OF GOD
	opposed it, including Charles Spurgeon. See principle of exclusion in Pendleton, p. 81, above.
9. The name Baptist Church The name non-essential.	1. Not in Bible. "Baptists" not in Bible. 2 John 9-11. 2. Acts 4:12: no other name. 3. Romans 7:1-4: Now married to Christ. Why wear John's name; he is only the friend of the Bridegroom.
10. Lord's Supper Non-immersed not allowed to commune. (Pendleton, p. 89, 90, 97). Observed monthly by Baptists.	1. 1 Corinthians 11:28: Examine self. 2. 1 Corinthians 5:12: God judges those without. Matthew 7. 3. Acts 20:7: first day of the week. (See 1 Corinthians 16:1-2) Acts 2:42.

Chapter Seven

CHURCHES OF CHRIST

Brief History:

"Churches of Christ trace their beginnings to the times of the apostles. Members believe that the first church of Christ was established on Pentecost after the resurrection and ascension of Jesus Christ. They claim that the church spread through the Roman world, but later declined."[1] Churches of Christ were restored in America through the efforts of Barton W. Stone in Kentucky (1803), James O'Kelley in the Carolinas (1794), Abner Jones and Elias Smith in New England around the turn of the century, and later Thomas Campbell (1808) of Virginia. Later, Alexander Campbell arrived from England (in 1809) and became a prominent leader in the restoration movement.[2] Groups in other countries have been discovered who are identical in doctrine and practice which also follow the New Testament as their only rule of faith and practice. This, they believe, is evidence that the work is of God, rather than being the product of a man-made set of traditions which produces denominations. They insist they are not a denomination.

Jesus Christ is regarded as founder, head and saviour of the church. They contend that the word of God is the seed of the kingdom, the church. When it is faithfully preached and obeyed without the addition of man's traditions or opinions, it will produce true Christians, collectively known as a church of Christ. They maintain that the New Testament sets forth faith, repentance, confession and baptism (immersion) as the conditions of salvation by Christ's blood.

There are about 18,000 independent churches of Christ. A group of elders oversee each church and a group of deacons serve. Most of the members are in the southern United States, with sizeable numbers in several foreign countries. They support about 500 family units in 75 foreign nations.[3] They have 6 affiliated senior colleges, some 20 junior colleges, more than 50 Bible teaching programs on university campuses. They support several orphanages and homes for the elderly. There are 120 known periodicals published by members of churches of Christ having a combined circulation of 1.6 million.[4] Total membership is estimated at 3 million.

>*Since no official source of authority or history is recognized by churches of Christ other than the New Testament scriptures, the traditions of men listed below will necessarily be limited to the record of the false teachings of human philosophy and wisdom recorded in that volume.

[1] B. C. Goodpasture, "Churches of Christ", World Book Encyclopedia, Volume 3, p. 423. - 1966 edition.

[2] Bill Humble, "Back To The Bible", Parts 2 and 3. Religious Services, Abilene, Texas.

[3] World Mission Information Bank, Webb Chapel Church of Christ, Dallas, Texas. 1980.

[4] Periodicals Published by Members of Churches of Christ, p. 27. 1975 edition.

TRADITIONS OF MEN	WORD OF GOD
1. Ananias and his wife discussed together and agreed to misrepresent the truth about a gift to the church. Obviously one first taught and the other accepted this error. This is the first sin in the church. False notions lead to false statements or teachings, yielding evil fruit in the lives of those involved. Acts 5:1-11.	1. Lying is not tolerated in the church. When a member of the church teaches falsely or is party to an untrue report, plan or doctrine, he (or she) lies not only to men but to God and the Holy Spirit. Acts 5:4, 9; Col. 3:9.
2. Simon thought and stated that the power of God, specifically to work miracles, could be bought with money, and suggested that a person other than an apostle could transmit such power to others by the laying on of hands. Acts 8:12-24.	2. This power cannot be bought with money. Acts 8:20. Only the apostles could transmit this power by the laying on of hands (Acts 8:14-18). Thus, after the apostles died, and those died upon whom they had laid hands, the power to work miracles came to an end.
3. Jewish Christians taught their brothers not to associate nor eat with Gentiles (uncircumcised men). Acts 11:2-3.	3. God through His Son upon the cross, broke down the barrier between Jew (the circumcised) and the Gentile (the uncircumcised), so that in the church of Christ there is no distinction or preference in race or national background. All are one in Christ. Acts 11:9; Gal. 6:15; Eph. 2:11-22; Rom. 3:21-30; 10:12.

4. Some Christians who were of the Pharisee sect of Jews said, "Except a man be circumcised after the manner of Moses, ye cannot be saved." Acts 15:5.

4. This is the same problem as in No. 3 above. To become a Christian, a person is not required to first become a Jew religiously by submitting to the requirements of Moses' law. Acts 15:2-33; Rom. 2:21-29.

5. The baptism of John was taught by Apollos at Ephesus. Acts 18:25.

5. Baptism by the authority ("in the name") of Jesus was the only baptism to be administered after the death, burial and resurrection of Christ. Matt. 28:18-20; Acts 2:38.

Early Christians therefore never wore the name of "John" or "Baptists". Believers who were baptized (immersed) into Christ (Rom. 6:3-4; Gal. 3:27) were added to Christ's church and wore only His name. Acts 2:47; 26:28; Col. 3:17; Phil. 2:10.

Those who were baptized erroneously as a result of a tradition of an uninformed or misguided preacher or teacher, should be baptized in water for the remission of sins by the authority of Christ. Acts 19:1-5.

6. Some Christians boasted of their secure position, not acknowledging that they had a debt to others, nor that they themselves could possibly fall away and be lost. Rom. 11:18.

6. It is possible for any branch (Christian) to fall away from grace into unbelief, and to be cut off by the severe justice of God. Rom. 11:22; Gal. 5:4; John 15:4-6.

7. Judging, despising and condemning others in the church over matters of indifference (such as eating meats or observing certain days), was a prevalent teaching. Rom. 14:1-5.

7. If a man regards a day, or eats, he does so with the full consent of his conscience (Rom. 14:5).
The feelings and conscience of others should be respected in matters which in themselves are neither right nor wrong. None lives "unto himself." Rom. 14:7-23.

8. Some made "fair speeches" and yet caused division because their words were not the true and pure doctrine of Christ. Rom. 16:17-18.

8. Hold fast the pattern of sound words and preach no other gospel. Titus 1:9-14; 2:1, 7-8; Gal. 1:6-9.
Strive for unity among all believers, based on true doctrine. Eph. 4:1-6.

9. Divisions within the body of Christ were promulgated by those who said they were "of" a certain preacher, wearing his name. 1 Cor. 1:10-12; 3:1-4.

9. Christ is not divided, nor is one baptized in the name of any man other than Christ. 1 Cor. 1:13-17; 3:5-10.

10. By teaching and promoting divisions on the basis or foundation of Peter or Paul, men were

10. The church is not built upon any man — only upon Christ. 1 Cor. 3:11-15, 21-23.

TRADITIONS OF MEN	WORD OF GOD
advocating a foundation other than Christ. 1 Cor. 3:11.	Men's person or teaching is not to be held above what is written. 1 Cor. 4:6.
11. The speech of some was proud and puffed up, discrediting the teachings of the apostles. 1 Cor. 4: 8-21.	11. The same things are to be taught everywhere in all the churches, not any man's gospel, but the doctrine of Christ alone, as delivered by the apostles. 1 Cor. 4:17; Jude 3.
12. Some in the church were glorying and puffed up over harboring immorality within the church. 1 Cor. 5:1, 2, 6.	12. Such teachings and attitudes must not be tolerated. The church was to have no company with such persons within the church. 1 Cor. 5:9-13.
13. It had become a practice among members of the church of Christ to take matters against each other into the civil courts. 1 Cor. 6:1-8.	13. Righteous men within the fellowship are to judge between brethren. It is better to take wrong than to enter lawsuits against brethren. 1 Cor. 6:5-8.
14. There is no resurrection of the dead. 1 Cor. 15:12, 35.	14. Christ was raised and all men will be raised for judgment and eternal rewards or punishment. John 5:28-29; 1 Cor. 15 The end (not the beginning of a reign upon earth) will come at Christ's return. 1 Cor. 15:23-24.
15. Many corrupt the word of God by false writing and teaching. 2 Cor.	15. The apostles Paul, Peter and other men inspired of the Holy Spirit only

TRADITIONS OF MEN	WORD OF GOD
2:17; 11:4; Gal. 1:6-9; 1 Tim. 1:3.	taught and wrote sincerely what was the word of the Lord. 1 Cor. 2:13; 2 Cor. 1:13; 2:14-17; 1 Peter 4:11; 2 Tim. 1:13; 4:1-4.
16. Some used themselves as a standard for comparison and for self commendation. 2 Cor. 10:12.	16. The standard for measuring is God's rule, the Scriptures, the word of Christ. 2 Cor. 10:13-18; John 12:48.
17. It is proper to do evil if good would come from it. Rom. 3:8.	17. It is never right to do wrong. Speak the truth in love. Eph. 4:15; 1 Thess. 5:22; 1 Tim. 2:7.
18. The resurrection is past already, taught by Hymanaeus and Philetus. 2 Tim. 2:18.	18. There are events yet to be fulfilled before the end comes. 2 Thess. 2:2-12; 1 Thess. 4:13-18.
19. Treat the poor with less honor and respect than the rich. James 2:2-3, 6.	19. There is to be no respect of persons with God. James 2:1, 4, 9.
20. Faith alone will save. James 2:14.	20. Acts of obedience must prove the genuineness of faith and the perfection of faith. Faith alone is dead. James 2:15-26.

Many other sins in the first century church could be ennumerated, most of which could be traced to following erroneous man-made teachings. Examples would include abuse of the Lord's Supper, women leading in assemblies, men demanding pre-eminence in ruling the church, etc.

Chapter Eight

ADVENTIST

Brief History:

Seventh Day Adventism originated in the movement of William Miller who set the time for the end of the world to be 1843. They now claim to be carrying on the work begun by Miller. Miller was a farmer who lived in Low Hampton, New York. When he was a Baptist (1831), he won 50,000 people to his views regarding the coming of Christ in 1843.

When this prophecy failed, he declared he had miscalculated and he then set the time at 1844 which also passed without incident. When he re-set it at 1845, some of his followers divided, and out of those fragments came Seventh Day Adventism. Adding some new doctrines (principally Sabbath keeping—Miller had observed Sunday as the Christian day of assembly), James White and his wife, Ellen G. White, became the leaders of the Sabbath branch of Adventism. She worte: "I have seen that the 1843 chart was directed by the hand of the Lord, and that it should not be altered; that the figures were as he wanted them; that his hand (was over and hid the mistake in some of the figures" (Early Writings, p. 64). "I saw that God was in the proclamation of the time 1843" (Spiritual Gift, Vol. I, p. 133). Mr. White also endorsed the Miller movement of Adventism (Life of Miller, p. 6). Mrs.

White further wrote: "As the churches refused to receive the first angel's message (Miller's work), they rejected the light of heaven and fell from the favor of God" (Early Writings, p. 101, quoted in Seventh Day Adventism Renounced by D. M. Canright, p. 68-69).

None of those who were later the leaders of Seventh Day Adventism such as White, Andrews, Bates and Rhodes were of any note in Miller's movement, though they were all in it. Yet afterwards, they claimed to be the only ones who had the right view of it, and all the rest were "in the dark," "foolish virgins," "apostates," etc. (Canright, p. 78-79). The word of Mrs. White came to be regarded as the voice of God. She claimed to have had visions emphasizing the importance of Sabbath observance, and Adventists regard her as a prophetess and her writings as inspired (see The Visions of Mrs. E. G. White, 144 pages. In this her inspiration is defended). Her writings are called Testimonies. "It is God and not an erring mortal, that has spoken" (Testimonies, Vol. III, p. 247. Those who oppose her are "not fighting against us, but against God," p. 260). Her last book is The Great Controversy.

ADVENTIST TRADITION	WORD OF GOD
1. "Law of God" and "Law of Moses". These are two different laws. Animal sacrifices and other ceremonies such as incense were in law of Moses and these only were taken away. God gave the Ten Commandments, and Moses gave ceremonies such as incense, etc.	1. One and the same law. Ezra 7:6,12. 2. Used interchangeably in Nehemiah 8:1,8; Luke 2:22-23. 3. God gave the law of Moses. Ezra 7:6. 4. Moses gave the law of God. 2 Chronicles 34:14. 5. Animal sacrifice was in the law of God. 2 Chronicles 31:3; Luke 2:24. 6. The law was changed. Hebrews 7:12. 7. Christ removed the first that he might establish the second. Hebrews 10:9-10. 8. "Moses said, Honor thy father and thy mother," the fifth of the Ten Commandments. Mark 7:10. Jesus said Moses gave it. 9. Killing forbidden in Ten Commandments, which Moses gave. John 17:19.
2. The Ceremonial Law only was nailed to the cross; The Ten Commandments were not part of the Ceremonial Law, hence not removed. The Ceremonial Law was the Book; the Moral law was on stone. Synopsis of Present Truth p. 255.	1. Only one law in Old Testament. 2 Chronicles 31:3; Nehemiah 8:2,3,8,14,18; Psalms 19:7; Malachi 4:4. 2. The "Book of the law" contained all five books of the Pentateuch. 1 Corinthians 14:34 refers to Genesis 3:16; Joshua 8:31 quotes Exodus 20:25; Ezra quotes Numbers 3:6; Matthew 22:36-40 quotes Levi-

ticus 19:18.

3. The "Book of the Law" by the ark quotes the Ten Commandments. Exodus 20:1-17; Deuteronomy 5:6-22.

4. Law of Lord contained both moral and ceremonial. 2 Chronicles 31:3; Matthew 22:36-40; Leviticus 19:1-37.

5. Moral things have to do with man's relationship to man and are right within themselves; ceremonial laws or religious laws are made right only by divine commandments and deal with man's relationship with God. Mark 2:27.

6. Ten Commandments done away. 2 Corinthians 3:7-11

7. Ten Commandments called covenant. Exodus 34:27-28; Deuteronomy 4:12; 13; 1 Kings 8:9,18; 2 Chronicles 5:10; 6:11.

8. Covenant of the decalogue abolished. Jeremiah 31:31-34; Zechariah 11:10-14; Hebrews 8:6-13; Hebrews 9:15-17.

9. Decalogue done away (consists of laws, statutes, commandments). Ephesians 2:15; Colossians 2:14-17.

10. The whole Law done away at the cross. Acts 15:1-11; Romans 6:14; 7:1-7;

ADVENTIST TRADITION	WORD OF GOD
	Galatians 3:23-25; 4:1-8; Hebrews 7:11-12.
3. The Sabbath is part of the Moral Law hence permanent.	1. Four of the 10 Commandments are "ceremonial" or "religious" in that they deal with relationship to God; six of the 10 are "moral" in that they deal with man's relationship with man. Sabbath law is not social, but religious. 2. Done away as part of Decalogue. 2 Corinthians 3:7-11. 3. Blotted out. Colossians 2:14-17; Hosea 2:11. Associated with meats, drinks, feast days. 4. Sabbath a shadow, supplanted by the substance. Hebrews 4:1-11; 10:1; Galatians 4:10, 11. 5. Apostles never taught Sabbath keeping, but did teach meeting on first day of the week. Acts 20:7; 1 Corinthians 16:1-2. 6. No meeting of Christians after the death of Christ was recorded as having been on a Sabbath day. 7. Paul's preaching was often to Jews on Sabbath in Synagogue in Acts. He preached, as did Christ, every day and every place. 8. All days of equal importance now. Romans 14:5.

ADVENTIST TRADITION	WORD OF GOD
	9. The Sabbath was commanded to Israel. Deuteronomy 5:15; Exodus 31:13-17.
	10. The Sabbath was a sign between God and Israel. (See reference above.)
4. The spirit in man is only his breath, which passes out of existence at death and is annihilated.	1. God is Spirit. John 4:24.
	2. We are God's offspring. Acts 17:28-29.
	3. God is totally immortal. 1 Timothy 6:16.
	4. God is Father of Spirits. Hebrews 12:9.
	5. Man is made of body and spirit; both mortal and immortal. Ecclesiastes 12:7; Acts 7:59; Luke 23:46.
	6. Departed spirits still exist and are conscious. Matthew 17:3—Moses and Elijah; 1 Samuel 22—Saul's spirit was brought forth and spoke; Matthew 22:32—Abraham living; Jehovah is God of living; Revelation 6:9-11—Souls of the dead were seen to be alive.
5. Ellen G. White's Testimonials are inspired like the Bible (See Testimonies, Vol. III, p. 257.)	1. 2 Peter 1:3: "All things" pertaining to life and godliness given in first century.
	2. Hebrews 1:1-2: God spoke through His Son, not through Ellen G. White, in these last days.

ADVENTIST TRADITION	WORD OF GOD
	3. Jude 3: The faith once for all delivered. 4. 2 Timothy 3:16 - 17: "Thoroughly furnished" by Scriptures.
6. Mrs. White made false prophecies: A. Impossible for slavery to be done away. <u>Testimonials,</u> Jan. 4, 1862, p. 256, 266.	1. If the prophecy come not to pass, it came not from God, do not hear him! Jeremiah 14:14ff. 2. Teach lies, the TAIL. Isaiah 9:15.
7. The Sabbath was kept by God, and that it has been kept by man from the creation.	1. Sabbath was "made known" to Moses. Nehemiah 9:14. 2. Duties of Sabbath: No fire—Exodus 35:3; No baking or boiling—Exodus 16:23; No travel—Exodus 16:29; Offer sacrifice—Numbers 28:9-10; No work—Exodus 20:9-10. 3. No record of any man keeping the Sabbath or knowing of it until Moses' time. It commemorated deliverance from Egypt. Deuteronomy 5:15; 1 Kings 8:9-21. 4. Not given to the fathers. Deuteronomy 5:1-14.
8. Catholics changed the Sabbath from Saturday to Sunday.	1. The Sabbath is still the Sabbath! No one changed it. 2. The law was changed by Christ before the Roman

ADVENTIST TRADITION	WORD OF GOD
	Catholic Church ever existed. Hebrews 7:12.
	3. Christians were taught not to keep the Sabbath. Colossians 2:16.
	4. Christ changed the day of worship, Hebrews 10:9-10, at the "time of reformation."
9. Observance of Lord's Supper at regular intervals is unimportant.	1. Early Christians observed weekly on first day of week. Acts 20:7; 2:42.

Chapter Nine

MORMONISM

Brief History:

The Church of Jesus Christ of Latter Day Saints, better known as the Mormon Church, was organized on April 6, 1830, at Fayette, New York, with six members by Joseph Smith, Jr.

Smith, following in the footsteps of his father as a roving water witch, became known as "Peep-stone Joe" because he claimed to have miraculously discovered a "peep-stone." At the age of fourteen he began to have visions and revelations. Being perplexed about the religious confusion of his day and the many conflicting denominations and their varied interpretations of the Scriptures, he said he received in the woods one day a vision of a great light. Instructions from God were not to join any of the sects, because God was about to restore the ancient gospel that had not been represented in its fulness by any of the churches existing at the time.

According to his statement, three years later he had a night vision in which Moroni, an angel, appeared before him and revealed to him the hiding place of certain plates of gold on which was inscribed the gospel. He was instructed by the angel to visit this place on the same date each year. September 22, 1827, he was permitted to receive the plates, at age 21.

He then translated the records, dictating the translation to Oliver Cowdery and others who wrote it down. It was completed in 1829 and placed in the hands of a printer in August, 1829. In the same year, on May 15, Smith and Cowdery said that an angel (John the Baptist) appeared to them and conferred upon them the Aaronic priesthood and commanded them to baptize each other by immersion. Later, three glorious personages (Peter, James and John) conferred the Melchizedek priesthood upon them and gave them the apostleship. These events were followed by the organization of the church at Fayette, April 6, 1830, with all its ancient gifts and powers.

Headquarters of the various churches that began to form was established in 1831 at Kirtland, Ohio. They met with rigid opposition in many areas, and were expelled from the state of Missouri in the winter of 1838-39. They then settled at Nauvoo, Illinois, but again hostility developed and Joseph Smith and his brother were killed at nearby Carthage, Illinois by a mob, June 27, 1844. Joseph Smith was shot to death in a jail, where he had been lodged on a charge of treason.

After Smith's death, Mormons split into several divisions.

In 1847, the Council of Twelve near Omaha, Nebraska, elected Brigham Young as President of the church. The main body of followers emigrated westward and settled in Utah. There have been various divisions, and today two main bodies exist. The "Reorganized" branch has headquarters at Independence, Missouri. This group rejects polygamy and the name Mormon; they do their own publishing. The branch that settled westward erected a magnificent Temple at Salt Lake City, and there situated the church headquarters. They claim three books to be inspired: The Pearl of Great Price, Doctrines and Covenants, and The Book of Mormon. Six temples have been erected in the U.S.A., the largest having been constructed on a 25 acre plot in Los Angeles at a cost of six million dollars.

1. God gave revelations of truth to Joseph Smith.

Considered to be the Word of God, the <u>Book of Mormon</u> is held as a companion book to the Bible. As stated by Joseph Smith in Article 8 of "Articles of Faith": "We believe the Bible to be the word of God, as far as it is translated correctly; we also believe the Book of Mormon to be the word of God." In addressing the 12 apostles, Joseph Smith said, "I told the brethren that the Book of Mormon was the most correct of any book on earth, and the keystone of our religion, and a man would get nearer to God by abiding by its precepts than by ANY other book" (A Compendium of the Doctrines of the Gospel, p. 273).

A Mormon apostle, Orson Pratt, said: "The nature of the Book of Mormon is such that, if true, no one can possibly be saved and reject it; if false, no one can possibly be saved and receive it." (Orson Pratt, Divine Authenticity of the Book of Mormon, p. 124)

The Book of Mormon is the word of God; then it is

1. The Faith Was Once Delivered.

The question now before us is whether revelation was complete and perfect in the 1st century or if there was still a vacuum or void left after the New Testament was given which was to be filled by a latter revelation.

Jude 3: "Beloved, while I was giving all diligence to write unto you of our common salvation, I was constrained to write unto you exhorting you to contend earnestly for THE FAITH WHICH WAS ONCE FOR ALL DELIVERED unto the saints." THE faith, not just any faith; not gradually being given through 2,000 years or given in part in the first century to be delivered again in the 19th century! O N C E DELIVERED. (Greek word here is "hapax," defined in Thayer's Lexicon as: "once, one time . . . never need repetition," also, "once for all"). The same word is employed in these verses: 2 Corinthians 11:25; Hebrews 9:26-28; 1 Peter 3:18.

2. The curse of heaven rests upon any man or angel or apostle who preaches any

to be accepted with equal authority . . . yea with GREATER authority, since it is not only the word of God, but translated into the English language by the power of God.

Joseph Smith

other gospel than that revealed in the New Testament (Galatians 1:8-9). Man is not to add to the words of the prophecy of this book as we read in Revelation 22: 18-19, nor to "go onward and abide not in the teaching of Christ" as we read at 2 John 9. Notice: "Seeing that his divine power HATH GRANTED unto us ALL THINGS THAT PERTAIN UNTO LIFE AND GODLINESS, through the knowledge of him that called us by his own glory and virtue." (2 Peter 1:3) We must conclude that since the divine power did not grant them the Book of Mormon, that it therefore does not "pertain unto life and godliness!"

3. "Every scripture inspired of God is also profitable for teaching, for reproof, for correction, for instruction which is in righteousness: that the MAN OF GOD MAY BE COMPLETE, FURNISHED COMPLETELY UNTO EVERY GOOD WORK." (2 Timothy 3:16-17) There is no room for later revelations; no vacuum; no need.

2. The man is a fool who says the Bible is sufficient and that it contains all of God's revealed truth, according to the Book of Mormon.

"And my words shall hiss forth unto the ends of the earth, for a standard unto my people, which are of the house of Israel; and because my words shall hiss forth—many of the Gentiles shall say: A Bible! A Bible! We have got a Bible, and there cannot be any more Bible. . . . Thou fool, that shall say: A Bible, we have got a Bible and we need no more Bible. Have ye obtained a Bible save it were by the Jews? . . . Wherefore, because that ye have a Bible ye need NOT SUPPOSE THAT IT CONTAINS ALL MY WORDS; neither need ye suppose that I have not caused more to be written... for out of the books which SHALL BE WRITTEN, I will judge the world. . . . For behold, I shall speak unto the Nephites and they shall write it; and I shall also speak unto the other tribes of the house of Israel, which I have led away, and they shall write it; and I shall also speak unto all nations of the

1. Deuteronomy 4:2; 12:32.
2. See above passages.
3. "Every good work" is recorded in the Bible, the Scriptures available in the first century (2 Timothy 3: 16-17).
4. The gospel was never "lost," hence absurd to speak of restoring its revelation. "My words shall never pass away," said Jesus (Matthew 24:35). What is new is not true; what is true is not new.

earth and they shall write it" (2 Nephi 29:2,3,6,10-12). Further, 2 Nephi 28:29 says "WO be unto him that shall say: We have received the word of God, and we need no more of the word of God, for we have enough!"

3. Translation of the Book of Mormon was "By the gift and power of God", hence not subject to human error.

a. "The prophet, scanning through the Urim and Thummim, the golden pages would appear in lieu of the strange characters thereon, their equivalent in English words. These he would repeat and a scribe, separated from him by a veil or curtain would write them down. Until the writing was CORRECT IN EVERY PARTICULAR, the words last given would remain before the eyes of the translater and not disappear. But, on the necessary corrections, being made, they would immediately pass away and be exceeded by others" (Brigham H. Roberts, The History of the Church, page 28).

b. "I will now give you a description of the manner in which the Book of Mormon was translated.

1. Fables and false prophets to be avoided. 1 Timothy 4:1; 2 Timothy 4:3-4. Joseph Smith was a base impostor, and the Book of Mormon a colossal fraud!

2. All liars shall be punished. Colossians 3:9; Revelation 21:8, 27; 22:15.

3. Men today should preach the same things taught in first century. 2 Timothy 2:2.

There is only one conclusion: the translation into the English language was absolutely perfect, and the ONLY flaws must be typographical or printer's errors. It is an undisputed fact, however, that there are even in the current editions many grammatical, historical, and literary errors which cannot be attributed as typographical!

Notice: "The book passed into a fluid condition and assumed a different FORM with every edition. In 1842

Joseph Smith would put the seer stone into a hat, and put his face in the hat, drawing it closely around his face to exclude the light; and in the darkness, the spiritual light would shine. A piece of something resembling parchment would appear, and under it was the interpretation in English. Brother Joseph would read off the English to Oliver Cowdery who was his principal scribe, and when it was written down and repeated to Brother Joseph to see if it was correct, then it would disappear, and another character with the interpretation would appear. Thus the Book of Mormon was translated BY THE GIFT AND POWER OF GOD, AND NOT BY THE POWER OF ANY MAN" (David Whitmer, An Address To All Believers In Christ, pp. 17f).

c. "The prophet possessed a seer stone which he was able to translate with as well as from the Urim and Thummim, and for convenience he then used the seer stone. By the aid of the seer stone, sentences would appear and were read by the prophet and written by

an edition appeared bearing on its title page the announcement, 'Carefully revised by the translator,' and such corrections have continued and accumulated so that 'a comparison of the latest Salt Lake edition with the first has shown more than three thousand changes'." (J. H. Snowden, The Truth About Mormonism, p. 69).

Martin Harris and when finished he would say, "Written," and if correctly written that sentence would disappear and another appear in its place. But, if not correctly written, it remained until corrected, so that the translation was JUST AS IT WAS ENGRAVEN ON THE PLATES PRECISELY IN THE LANGUAGE THEN USED" (Martin Harris, The Myth of the Manuscripts Found, p. 91).

d. "And we know that they (the golden plates) have been translated by the gift and power of God, for his voice hath declared it unto us; wherefore we know of a surety that the work is true"

(Oliver Cowdery, David Whitmer, and Martin Harris, Testimony of the Three Witnesses, in Book of Mormon preface.

MORMON TRADITION	WORD OF GOD

4. Characters were of an ancient language:

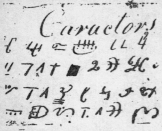

Characters Suppose To Have Been
On The Golden Plates

1. Prove all things. 1 Thessalonians 5:21.

The Egyptian hieroglyphics in 1833 had not been fully deciphered, and there was no way of proving Smith's work. However, in 1861 Smith's translation was shown to a scholar named Theodule Deveria of Paris, who declared the work was "entirely incorrect." So also attest eight other distinguished scholars in Egyptian lore (Snowden, Ibid., pp. 76-79).

5. Some grammatical and language blunders and absurdities in the Book of Mormon:

1. God is not the author of confusion. 1 Corinthians 14:33.

1830 Edition

p. 193 "the priests was"
p. 192 "They was added"
p. 290 "they did not fight against God no more"
p. 351 "that all might see

the writing which he had wrote upon the rent"

p. 506 "I have wrote them" "I were about to write" "that to teach baptism unto they"

p. 582 "this t h i n g had ought not to be"

p. 224 "and this he done"

1949 Edition

2 Nephi 33:4—"the words... it"

Words of Mormon 1:2—"it supposeth me"

Moroni 9:5—"it seemeth me"

I Nephi 6:2—"we are a descendant of Joseph"

Alma 13:1—"I would cite your minds forward to the time when the Lord God gave"

Alma 14:6—"his soul began to be harrowed up"

Alma 24:17—"they did bury them up deep in the earth"

Helaman 9:6—"Now, Immediately when the judge had been murdered—he being stabbed by his brother by a garb of secrecy" (a strange weapon!)

Ether 2:17—"t h e length thereof was the length of a tree" (see verses 16-25)

Ether 3:1—"the brother of Jared . . . did molten" (ad-

Does this sound like the product of "the gift and

jective should be replaced by the verb, melt)

6. Book of Mormon refutes any claim to inspiration. I Nephi 1:3—"I make it according to MY knowledge"

Nephi wrote what his knowledge led him to write, and only what "I think it to be sacred" (I Nephi 19:6). Hear him again: "And now if I do err" (I Nephi 19:6).

Now let us hear Jacob: "I should write . . . which I considered to be most precious" (Jacob 1:2). He concludes saying, "I have written according to the best of my knowledge" (Jacob 7:26). What they <u>thought</u> was true according to <u>their</u> knowledge, <u>if</u> they do not err!!!

Also see 3 Nephi 8:1-2 and Mormon 8:12—"if there was no mistake made by this man," and "because of the imperfections which are in it (this record)." They wrote "according to my <u>memory</u>" (Ether 5:1).

7. Some contradictions between the Book of Mormon and the Bible:
    a. I Nephi 19:10—Darkness at Jesus' death.

power of God?" GOD IS NO SUCH IGNORAMUS!

1. Those who "oppose themselves" should be corrected and instructed. 2 Timothy 2:25. The writers of the Book of Mormon claim they are inspired in one place, and not inspired in another.

1. Matthew 27:45.
2. Matthew 2:1. In Bethlehem, about 7 miles out of Jerusalem.

b. Jesus born at Jerusalem —Alma 7:10.

c. Disciples called Christians first 73 B.C.—Alma 46: 13-14.

d. Church of Christ built about 147 B.C.—Mosiah 18: 17.

e. Mysteries unfolded 600 B.C.—I Nephi 10:19.

f. Seer is greater than a prophet.—Mosiah 8:15.

g. The Lord's Supper is a common meal to "fill" the participants—3 Nephi 18:8. Followers of Book of Mormon do not obey it, for they take water and bread—3 Nephi 18:13.

h. Priests outside the tribe of Levi—2 Nephi 5:26. (Yet, 2 Nephi 5:10 says they kept the Law of Moses "in all things.")

i. Men have authority in the church—Mosiah 26:8, 37.

j. Melchizedek had a father—Alma 13:18.

8. The fall of Adam and Eve was "one of the great steps to eternal exaltation and happiness and one ordered of God."
Catechism for Children, p. 33.

3. Acts 11:26. First in Antioch about 45 A.D.
4. Matthew 16:18. 33 A.D.

5. Ephesians 3:4-5; Matthew 13:17. Not until days of apostles, first century A.D.
6. 1 Samuel 9:9. Same.
7. 1 Corinthians. 11:20-22. The meal was separate from Lord's Supper. Matthew 26:26-29.

8. Numbers 3:9,10. Hebrews 8:4.

9. Ephesians 1:22-23; Colossians 1:18. Christ has all authority in the church.
10. Hebrews 7:3. He had none.

Genesis 3:19; Romans 5: 12-18; Romans 6:1-2. Disobedience to God's law has never been His desire or "order."

MORMON TRADITION	WORD OF GOD
9. Joseph Smith contradicts himself on doctrine of polygamy.	1. Sinners and false teachers "oppose themselves."
a. Polygamy of David and Solomon "which thing was abominable before me, saith the Lord."	
Book of Mormon, Jacob 2:24.	
b. God gave David all his wives and concubines "by the hand of Nathan, my servant, and others of the prophets . . . " He sinned in none of these things except in the case of Uriah and his wife.	
Doctrines and Covenants, 132:39.	
10. Polygamy is a command to obey and if disobeyed, damnation is the penalty.	1. **Man is to cleave to his wife, not wives. Genesis 2** 18-25.
The Seer, Vol. 1, p. 158.	2. Man has one wife, Ephesians 5:23-33, the same as Christ has one church.
Doctrines and Covenants, 132:3, 4, 6, 61, 62.	3. Elders must be husband of one wife. 1 Timothy 3:2.
	4. Lamech, a murderer, originated polygamy. Genesis 4:19-24.
11. There are many gods, "a general assembly, quorum or grand council of the gods, with their president at their head, constitute the designing and creating power."	1. Only one God. Genesis 1:26; Exodus 20:1-3; Matthew 28:19; John 1:1-3; 14:25-26; 16:7-10.
Key of Theology, p. 52.	

12. Doctrine of God:

a. God in heaven "has flesh and bones. The Father has a body of flesh and bones as tangible as man's."

Doctrines and Covenants, 130:22.

b. He has sex and marries and multiplies His species. "God, angels, and men are all of one great species, one race, one great family."

Key of Theology, p. 41, 52.

The Seer, Vol. 1, p. 37.

c. Adam is God, and Eve was "one of his wives."

Pearl of Great Price, p. 60.

Journal of Discourses, Vol. 6, p. 50.

d. "God himself was once as we are now and is an exalted man."

Journal of Discourses, Vol. 6, p. 3, sermons by Joseph Smith.

13. Doctrine of Christ:

a. Christ is Adam's son by natural generation. "He was not begotten by the Holy Spirit. And who is the Father? He is the first of the human family."

Journal of Discourses, Vol. 1, p. 50, sermon by Brigham Young.

b. Jesus was a polygamist.

1. God is spirit. John 4:24; 1 Corinthians 15:50.

2. A spirit has not flesh and bones. Luke 24:39.

3. God is omnipresent. Psa. 139:7-11; Acts 17:28; 1 Corinthians 3:16.

4. God's only marriage relationship was spiritual, with Israel. Jeremiah 3:14.

5. No marriage after death. Mark 12:25.

6. Adam is not God, but was created by Him. Genesis 1:27; 2:18-25; 3:8-11, 19; Exodus 20:1-3.

7. Man is a created being. Genesis 2:7.

8. Christ was like us only from his fleshly aspect after he came to earth. Isaiah 7:14; Matthew 1:20-23.

1. Jesus was conceived of the Holy Spirit. Isaiah 7:14; Matthew 1:18-23.

2. Christ is the one husband and head of his one bride, the church. John 3:29; Romans 7:4; Ephesians 5:23-33.

". . . there were several holy women that greatly 'loved Jesus, such as Mary and Martha her sister, and Mary Magdalene; and Jesus greatly loved them . . . if all the acts of Jesus were written, we, no doubt, should learn that these beloved women were His wives."

The Seer, Vol. 1, p. 158-159.

14. Doctrine of The Holy Spirit:

Not a person, but ethereal substance, pure and refined.

1. Holy Spirit is a person, one of the three persons in the godhead. Matthew 28:19; John 14:15-17; 16:13-14; Acts 5:3-4; 8:29; 10:19-20.
2. He is not a mysterious "it," but a personal "He."

15. Doctrine of Apostles:

a. Twelve apostles were appointed by David Whitmer and Oliver Cowdery:

T. B. Marsh, Parley Pratt, D. W. Patten, Luke Johnson, Brigham Young, Wm. Smith, H. C. Kimball, Orson Pratt, Orson Hyde, John Boynton, Wm. M'Lellin, Lyman Johnson.

b. They maintain an apostleship in the church.

1. Those claiming apostleship tried and "found them liars." Revelation 2:2.
2. Apostles had to be eyewitnesses of the Lord "from the baptism of John." Acts 1:25. Saul was "the last of all" chosen as apostle who "saw the Lord." Acts 9:6; 22:17-21; 1 Corinthians 15:8.
3. Apostles cannot exist today because none can do the signs of an apostle, and none living today has seen the Lord.

16. Doctrine of Salvation:

a. Salvation is the resurrection from the dead.

Doctrines and Covenants, 88:16.

b. Salvation consists of 3 degrees: highest or celestial, terrestrial (deceived, etc.), and those who did not accept Mormonism, liars, sorcerers, etc.

Doctrines and Covenants, 76:51-112.

1. Both good and bad will be resurrected. John 5:28-29; Revelation 20:11-15.

2. Universal salvation is not taught in the Scriptures. Matthew 25.

3. Matthew 25:46. Only eternal life or eternal punishment.

4. Revelation 22:4.

17. Baptism for the Dead:

The saints can be baptized for those who have died.

Doctrines and Covenants, 124:28.

Journal of Discourses, Vol. 6, p. 7-8, Joseph Smith.

1. Man must be baptized by his own faith and volition. Romans 6:3-4, 17-18; Acts 2:37-38.

2. A man is "dead in sin" before he is baptized, hence is baptized for the old dead self. See 1 Corinthians 15:29. Responsible only for deeds done in own body. 2 Corinthians 5:10.

3. There is no second chance after death. Luke 16:19-31; Acts 17:31.

18. "Every spirit that confesses that Joseph Smith is a prophet . . . and that the Book of Mormon is true, is of God, and every spirit that does not is of "Antichrist."

Millenial Star, Vol. 5, p. 118, by Brigham Young.

1. Confess Christ, not Joseph Smith. Matthew 10:32-33; Romans 10:9-10.

2. Many false prophets. Matthew 7:15; 24:11; 2 Corinthians 11:13; 2 Peter 2:1; 1 John 4:1.

Chapter Ten

JEHOVAH'S WITNESSES

Brief History:

The organizer of this movement was Charles Taze Russell (1854-1916). He embraced Adventism early in life, but at the age of 20 abandoned it primarily due to his opinion that the date fixed by Wm. Miller for the second coming of Christ was erroneous. He insisted that the date of the second advent was 1874, the same year he began to preach (Studies in the Scriptures, Vol. II, p. 240). In our opinion, it seemed not to matter to him that Jesus had said that neither the Son nor the angels knew, but "the Father only" (Mark 13:32).

"Pastor" Russell formally organized his followers in Pittsburgh in 1872, with himself as President. Headquarters were moved to Brooklyn, New York, in 1909. It is reported that about 13,000,000 of Russell's Studies in the Scriptures (Volumes 1-6) have been circulated. These laid the foundation for the new sect known before 1931 as Millennial Dawnists, International Bible Students, and Russellites.

In his six volumes (he prophesied he would write seven, but death overtook him before the task was finished) he maintained that the plan of God was unfolded and made known through him "as never before," and added that "the opening of the books of divine revelation will soon be completed"

(Vol. 2, p. 189). In addition to this claim of "divine revelation," Russell maintained that probably never before had anyone (this would include the apostles!) "understood any part" of the book of Revelation (I, p. 27).

It is the old story of an ambitious man claiming that the Bible truths are hidden "from all except the consecrated" (Finished Mystery, p. 65), and saying, "Lo! Here is my writing, the long-awaited true explanation."

Charles Taze Russell's first book was published in 1886 which he entitled Millennial Dawn. The name was changed to Studies in the Scriptures in 1916, but the disciples of Russell came to be known in the early stages of the movement as "Millennial Dawnists," "Russellites," or "International Bible Students."

After 'Pastor' Russell's death in 1916, his adherents were slowly culled out and pushed out of the newer organization now headed by Judge Rutherford. Russell's old Watchtower Society passed into oblivion by federal court order in 1918. Finally, with all of Russell partisans out of the way, it was evident to all of Rutherford's adherents that a new name would have to be selected. This new name was given at a convention held at Columbus, Ohio, October, 1931 (Theocracy, p. 34). The new name, Jehovah's Witnesses, identified the new sect headed by Rutherford.

In an effort to cover up the newness of the name, it was contended that Jehovah had witnesses from the time of Abel, and that Isaiah 62:2 prophesied the giving of the new name in 1931. Each issue of the Watchtower magazine carries these words on the cover: "You are my witnesses, says Jehovah—Isaiah 43:12."

Without the Watchtower hierarchy, the slaves would pass into oblivion as sheep without a shepherd . . . and this is precisely what the Watchtower said would happen to a man who lays Russell's books down and reads the Bible only! "Within two years he goes into darkness!" (September 10, 1910, p. 298).

Today, the Watchtower Bible and Tract Society with main headquarters in Brooklyn, N. Y., prints over 100 million copies of their material in some 80 languages each year.

RUSSELLISM TRADITION	WORD OF GOD
1. 'Jehovah's Witnesses' used as a name since 1931.[1]	1. Never used as a name. 1 Peter 4:16.
2. Have earthly headquarters in New York with president, etc., etc.[2]	2. God praised through the church only. Ephesians 3: 10, 21.
3. Charles T. Russell, founder, received revelation of truths heretofore unknown. Scripture Studies, Vol. I, pp. 20 & 28.[3]	3. Apostles guided into ALL truth. John 16:13; 2 John 9-11.
4. 'Cannot see the divine plan in studying the Bible itself'; without books Russell wrote a person goes into darkness within two years. Watchtower, Sept. 15, 1910, p. 298.[4] "But we see, also that if anyone lays the Scripture Studies aside (Russell's books), even after he has read them for ten years—if he lays them aside and ignores them and goes to the Bible alone, though he has understood the Bible for ten years, our experience shows that within two years he goes into darkness." Watchtower Sept. 15, 1910.	4. 2 Timothy 3:16-17; Ephesians 1:3; 2 Peter 1:3.

1. Theocracy, page 34 (one of their books).
2. Not disputed. See ch. 4, 30 Yrs. Watchtower Slave.
3. Studies in the Scriptures, I, 20, 28.
4. Watchtower, September 15, 1910, p. 298.

5. No man has or possesses a soul. [5]	5. Luke 21:19; 1 Thessalonians 5:23; James 1:21.
6. Wicked will not be raised with the righteous. [6]	6. In the same hour all will come forth from the tombs. John 5:28-29.
7. Christ's 2nd coming 'invisible' and only to a few persons. SS, II, p. 153.[7]	7. All, every eye shall see Him. Revelation 1:7.
8. Jesus was the first creature.[8]	8. Never called creature, but He is Creator of all things. John 1:1; Colossians 1:16; Romans 1:25.
9. Jesus not divine while in the flesh but only human. SS, I, p. 179.[9] "In truth, when Jesus was on earth He was a perfect man, nothing more and nothing less." (Reconciliation, page 111).	9. Jesus repeatedly accepted worship as God during earthly ministry, but good men did not. Matthew 8:2; Matthew 1:23; John 1:14; Acts 14.
10. Jesus' body not raised but preserved somewhere or dissolved into gases. (Deliverance, p. 170; The Time Is At Hand, p. 129).[10]	10. Matthew 28:5-6; Luke 24:39; Acts 2:31-32. God raised up the same Jesus.

---

5. Reconciliation, p. 293.
6. Children, p. 361.
7. Studies in the Scriptures, II, p. 153.
8. Make Sure of all Things, p. 207.
9. also Reconciliation, p. 111.
10. Deliverance, p. 170; also The Time Is At Hand, p. 129.

RUSSELLISM TRADITION	WORD OF GOD
"Somewhere Jehovah miraculously preserved that body." (Deliverance, page 170. This is another of Rutherford's books.).	
11. Jesus no longer a man after the resurrection, but a spirit creature. [11]	11. The man Christ Jesus is today our Mediator. 1 Timothy 2:5.
12. Holy Spirit is not a person, but the active force of God. [12]	12. He is a person: speaks, hears, r e s i s t s, comforts, wills, guides. John 16:13; Romans 8:26; Is God, Acts 5:3-4. Cf. Romans 15:19, power and Spirit are distinct.
13. There is no godhead consisting or composed of three persons. [13]	13. Colossians 2:9; Matthew 28:19; 2 Corinthians 13:14.
14. Christ's kingdom not fully established in AD 33. The church is not the kingdom. [14]	14. Mark 9:1; Colossians 1:13. The church is the kingdom. Hebrews 12:23-28; Matthew 16:18-19.
15. The earth will never be destroyed. [15]	15. Matthew 24:35; 2 Peter 3:10—Earth AND works therein to burn up, dissolve, pass away.

11. Reconciliation, p. 298; St. in Scrip, V, p. 362.
12. Make Sure of All Things, p. 364; Reconciliation, p. 115, 116.
13. Reconciliation, p. 100, 101.
14. Make Sure of All Things, p. 234; The Truth Shall Make You Free, p. 240; St. in the Scrip., I, p. 73.
15. Make Sure of All Things, p. 108.

RUSSELLISM TRADITION	WORD OF GOD
16. Instruments of music used in worship.[16]	16. Not authorized. Matthew 15:7-9. Singing only, Ephesians 5:19, etc.
17. Lord's Supper only once a year.[17]	17. Weekly, first day of week. Acts 20:7.
18. Baptism called a 'dedication' 66 times in Watchtower, July 1, '55; baptism has nothing to do with the remission of sins.[18]	18. Acts 2:38; 22:16; 1 Peter 3:21. It is never called a dedication; is 'for remission of sins.'
19. Baptism does not put one into Christ, His body, the church.[19]	19. Galatians 3 : 27; Romans 6:3-4.
20. The wicked will not suffer eternal punishment in hell.[20]	20. Matthew 25:46; 10:28.
21. There is no consciousness after physical death.[21]	21. 1 Samuel 28:7-19; Luke 16:19ff; Matthew 17:3—not a fable, 2 Peter 1:16-18.
22. A second chance to hear the gospel after this life is over.[22]	22. Luke 16:19ff; Acts 1:25; John 8:21-24; Revelation 22:11; Acts 17:30.
23. Hell is only the grave.[23]	23. **Mark 9:43-48**: **Psalms 9**: 17. Then only the wicked are to be buried!

16. Not disputed.
17. Announcements in various issues of the Watchtower; not disputed.
18. Make Sure, p. 30.
19. Watchtower, July 1, 1955, p. 402, 1st column.
20. Make Sure, p. 162; Enemies, p. 127-8.
21. Creation, p. 204.
22. Divine Plan of the Ages, p. 305; Make Sure of All Things, p. 322, 323.
23. Reconciliation, p. 28; Let God Be True, p. 91.

RUSSELLISM TRADITION	WORD OF GOD
24. The church is to have exactly 144,000, no more; already filled.[24]	24. All the saved are added to the church of Christ, Acts 2:47; Ephesians 5:23. God still saves all who believe and obey Christ, Mark 16:15-16; Hebrews 5:8-9, until the end.
25. Hope to live on earth.[25]	25. Heavenly hope, 1 Peter 1:3-4; Colossians 3:1-2; 1 John 2:15. Only ONE hope according to Ephesians 4:4.
26. No collections on first day of the week.[26]	26. 1 Corinthians 16:1-2.
27. Gospel has never been preached to the w h o l e world.[27]	27. Colossians 1:6, 23, every creature heard.
28. Russell prophesied that after 1914 there would be no Odd Fellowship, Free Masonry, trade unions, guilds, trusts 'and societies secular and ecclesiastical,' nor navies and armies. SS, II, 139; VI, 633.[28]	28. All false prophets condemned, Deuteronomy 18: 21-22; Revelation 20:10, tormented day and night for ever and ever.

---

24. Harp of God, p. 191.
25. Make Sure, p. 108f.
26. Not disputed.
27. The Kingdom Is At Hand, p. 316, 344; This Means Everlasting Life, p. 214; Let God Be True, p. 141. Inferred in all these.
28. St. in Scrip., II, p. 139; VI, p. 633.

RUSSELLISM TRADITION	WORD OF GOD
29. Russell o n c e taught that Christ returned to earth in 1874, but now the date has been changed to 1914![29]	29. The Watchtower contradicts itself as well as the Bible. Mr. F. W. Franz, their V. Pres., admitted this anachronism in 1954 in the courts of Scotland.

29 Russell's book, St. in the Scrip., I, p. iii, says certain thought "formerly immaturely seen" was "changed" in later edition of his book. Article in Firm Foundation tells of the court trial where Mr. Franz admitted the change in dates. St. in Scrip., II, p. 240. See also The Harp of God, p. 237, 244.

Chapter Eleven

CHRISTIAN SCIENCE

Brief History:

A mental healer by the name of Dr. Quimby appeared early in the nineteenth century in Portland, Maine. He made experiments in healing by hypnotism and mesmerism. One of his students was a Mrs. Mary Baker Glover Patterson Eddy, who from 1862 to 1865 had attracted some notoriety as a mesmeric subject.

One year after Dr. Quimby died (1865), Mrs. Eddy claimed to have received a revelation in which she received a discovery of the doctrines of Christian Science. She wrote these philosophies down in a book entitled Science and Health, strikingly similar to a book authored by Dr. Quimby, Science of Man. Mrs. Eddy copyrighted her book and sold it in several editions at handsome revenues. The first edition appeared in 1875, followed by many editions containing many changes . . . Science and Health With Key To The Scriptures.

The first Science and Health Association was organized in 1876 with six pupils. The first Science Church was established by her in Boston in 1879 with twenty-six members. She was the pastor of this, the "Mother Church." All other churches of this connection are branch churches of the mother church. Membership has always run about three women to every man.

"Church of Christ, Scientist" is the official church name.

Mrs. Eddy's career was a checkered one, having thrice married and once divorced. She reaped a financial fortune; despite her insistence that nothing material is real, she amassed a worth of over three million dollars by the time of her death in 1910. She had said, "There is no death."

Mary Baker Eddy

CHR. SCIENCE TRADITION	WORD OF GOD
1. Mary Baker Eddy is the head of the church, and was its first pastor in Boston. (See Historical Sketch).	1. Jesus is the "only potentate." 1 Timothy 6:14-15. 2. Jesus is the only head of the church. Ephesians 1:20-23. 3. Pastors (elders) in the scripture were required to be 'the husband of one wife.' 1 Timothy 3; Titus 1. How could she be a husband at all? 4. Women are limited in their participation in public church assemblies to a place of subjection and silence. 1 Corinthians 14:34; 1 Timothy 2:12.
2. The Bible is not pure, defiled by material and moral senses. (Eddy, Science and Health, 139:20-22).	1. Proverbs 30:5. 2. Romans 3:4. 3. 2 Timothy 3:16. 4. 2 Peter 1:21; Matthew 24:35. 5. The word of God is perfect. James 1:25.
3. The church originated in Boston in 1876.	1. Scriptures teach that Jerusalem is where the church was established. Isaiah 2:3; Luke 24:47; Acts 2:1-47. 2. Scriptures teach that the time was when power came and when the Spirit came—the first Pentecost after the resurrection of Christ. Joel 2; Acts 2; Mark 9:1; Acts 1:8.

3. Every plant which the Father did not plant shall be rooted up. Matthew 15:13.

4. "A Christian Scientist is one who accepts and practices Christian Science as a religion."

George Channing, "What Is A Christian Scientist?"

Leo Rosten, Religions of America, p. 21.

1. Paul once referred to "science falsely so-called." 1 Timothy 6:20-21. These have erred from the faith of Christ.
2. Mary Baker Eddy's religion was neither Christian nor truly scientific.

5. The name, "Church of Christ, Scientists"

—on all buildings a n d literature.

1. Jesus referred to the church as "My church." Matthew 16:18.
2. It was purchased with His blood. Acts 20:28.
3. Paul, referring to various congregations, said: "The churches of Christ." Romans 16:16.

6. Mrs. Eddy "reinstated primitive Christianity and its lost element of healing."

Religious Bodies, Statistics, History and Doctrines, Vol. II, p. 397ff.

"I must know the science of this healing, and I won my way to absolute conclusions through divine revelations, reason, and demonstration."

Science and Health, p. 109.

1. Those who are physically sick have need of a physician. Matthew 9:12.
2. Jesus healed miraculously and even raised from the dead, but told His disciples they would do "greater works." John 14:12. What is greater than healing the sick or restoring sight to the blind? It is saving the souls of men through the preaching of the good news of the death, burial and resurrection of Jesus Christ. 1 Corinthians 15:1-4. This greater

work could later be done because Jesus said, "I go to my Father."

3. Physical miraculous healing, drinking deadly poison, etc., was performed by Christ and His apostles for the specific purpose of confirming the word. Hebrews 2:1-4; Mark 16:20.

4. All revelation of truth was complete in the first century. Jude 3 ("The faith was once for all delivered to the saints.")

5. Once fully revealed, confirmed by signs, and recorded by competent witnesses, the truth was completely delivered and there was no longer a need for confirming that truth again and again.

7. God is "harmonious mind-action," divine, infinite mind, principle, truth.
   Science and Health, 109: 16-17; 465:8-10.

1. God is a person. Genesis 1:1-31; Hebrews 1:3.

8. Jesus Christ is not God, except in same sense that "God and man, Father and Son, are one in being."
   Science and Health, 36: 12-18.

1. Jesus is God. Isaiah 9:6; John 20:28; Philippians 2:5-6; Hebrews 1:8.

He was not incarnated in the flesh: "The Virgin Mary conceived this idea of God,

2. Jesus became flesh. Luke 1:30, 31, 34, 35; John 1:14; Luke 24:39.

and gave to her ideal the name of Jesus."

Science and Health, 29: 14-18.

Christ and Jesus are two: "Christ is the ideal truth; Jesus is the name of the man who more than all other men has presented Christ, the true idea of God . . . Jesus is the human man and Christ is the divine idea; hence the duality of Jesus the Christ."

Science and Health, 475: 10-17.

3. Jesus is the Christ. Matthew 16:16-18.
4. The same person, in fleshly body. John 20:31; Romans 5:8; 1 Corinthians 15: 3; 1 Peter 1:19; Ephesians 2:13-16.
5. A man is a liar (so is a woman!) who does not confess Jesus is the Christ, one and the same. 2 John 7.
6. Jesus Christ is come in the flesh. 2 John 7.

Jesus did not die.
Science and Health, 46: 2, 3; 44:28-29; 45:11-12.

7. He did die. John 19:33; Romans 5:8; 14:9; 15:3; 1 Corinthians 15:1-4; and many others.

Jesus did not rise from the dead physically.
Science and Health, 313: 26-30.

8. He did arise physically. Luke 24:39-43; John 20:26-29.

The "material blood of Jesus" will not save from sin.
Science and Health, 25: 6-9.

9. We are saved from sin by the blood of Christ. Romans 5:9; Colossians 1:20; Hebrews 10:4-12; 1 John 1:7.

[Note: This is an admission that Jesus is the Christ and that He came in the flesh and that physical blood ran through His veins.]

9. The Holy Spirit is "divine science."

Science and Health, 55: 27-29.

Cannot dwell in a body.
Science and Health, 309: 24-25.

1. The Spirit dwells in us. 1 Corinthians 3:16; 6:19; 2 Timothy 1:14.

10. There are not three persons in the one God, or Godhead.

Science and Health, 515: 17-19.

1. "Let us make man." Genesis 1:26.
2. Three persons: Matthew 28:19.

11. Sin, sickness and death are illusions.

Science and Health, 283: 8-11.

"Man is incapable of sin, sickness and death."

Science and Health, 475: 28.

"Lazarus never died."

Science and Health, 575: 413.

"Man is never sick."

Science and Health, 393: 29.

"There is no disease."

Science and Health, 421: 18.

"Death an illusion."

Science and Health, 584: 9.

1. All men sin. 1 Kings 8: 46; Romans 3:23; Luke 7: 47.
2. If we say we have no sin, we lie. 1 John 1:8-9.
3. See Matthew 4:24; Mark 6:5; John 4:46.
4. Man has died since Adam. Genesis 5:1-5.
5. "Lazarus is dead." John 11:14.
6. Men must die by God's decree. Hebrews 9:27.

12. Divorce is acceptable by mutual consent or by legal dissolution.

Miscellaneous Writings, 297:18-25.

1. Divorce allowable only on one condition. Matthew 5: 31-32; Matthew 19:8-9.

CHR. SCIENCE TRADITION	WORD OF GOD
13. Christian Science abolishes Baptism and the Lord's Supper from their practice.	1. Christ commands baptism and promises salvation from sin to all who by faith obey it. Matthew 28:18-19; Mark 16:15-16; Acts 2:38; Galatians 3:26-27. 2. The Lord's Supper was observed weekly by Christians from t h e apostolic times. Acts 2:42; 20:7; 1 Corinthians 11:23-29; John 6:53 (No life except we eat Christ's flesh and drink his blood in remembrance).
14. "If prayer nourishes the belief that sin is cancelled, and that man is made better merely by praying, prayer is an evil." Science and Health, p. 5.	1. Men should pray everywhere. 1 Timothy 2:8. 2. Men should pray in everything Philippians 4:6. 3. Men should pray always. 1 Thessalonians 5:17.

Recommended reading:
The Christian Science Myth
by Martin & Klann

Chapter Twelve

PENTECOSTALISM

Brief History:

"The Pentecostal Church, Inc., traces its beginning to New Years Eve, 1899. In Topeka, Kansas, a band of earnest hungry-hearted Christian people, being hungry for more of God, called a fast that lasted twenty-one days. During this time they prayed earnestly for a great outpouring of the Holy Spirit, which to their joyful surprise came at midnight on New Years Eve, 1899. Mighty manifestations were witnessed in the meeting soon after midnight, and people were heard speaking in other languages as the Holy Spirit gave utterance in the same manner as the 120 received it on the Day of Pentecost, when the multitudes came together and they were understood to speak in the different languages of the earth . . . "

"Ministers and evangelists came from every section of the United States and missionaries returned from the foreign field to learn more about this strange doctrine. Many who came received a like experience of the group in Topeka, and returned to their field of labor preaching that Jesus Christ is the same yesterday, today, and forever . . . . But in the year 1914 a conference was called at Hot Springs, Ark., during which a General Council of the Assemblies of God was formed. Later because of what many believed to be new revelation of doctrine this group was divided and two or three other smaller groups soon formed, among them being what is known as The Pentecostal Church, Inc., was formed, composed of white brethren only." (Religious Bodies. Statistics, History and Doctrines, Vol. II, p. 1334-5, quoted in Modern Churches and The Church, p. 205.)

"During the last twenty-one days of the nineteenth century a band of earnest, hungry-hearted ministers and Christian workers in Bethel Bible College, Topeka, Kansas, called a fast, praying earnestly for a great outpouring of the Holy Spirit, which, to their joyful surprise, came upon them in the early hours of the morning, on January 1, 1900 . . . In the year 1914 came the revelation on the name of the Lord Jesus Christ. The pivotal doctrines of the absolute deity of Jesus Christ and baptism in his name became tenets of faith. God marvelously confirmed our message as the Gospel was preached in its fulness. The power which was hidden in the name of Jesus began to be revealed. Literally thousands were rebaptized into the name of Jesus Christ, and multitudes received the baptism of the Holy Spirit while in the water.

"Great numbers were healed of incurable diseases; demons were cast out as in the days of the apostles. In many cities where this message had gone, the report of the Samaritan revival was duplicated. (Acts 8:12) . . . .

"During the early half of this century various groups were organized. Among them two of the major bodies known as the Pentecostal Assemblies of Jesus Christ, Inc., and the Pentecostal Church, Inc., became so closely associated in doctrine and fellowship that in 1944 steps were taken to unite the two bodies into one organization known as the United Pentecostal Church . . . . To this end we now pledge our prayers, our faith, our life, and love, our earthly means of support, and our times, in the fear of God and for his glory alone. UNITED PENTECOSTAL CHURCH." (Pentecostal Church Manual, pp. 8-10, Foreword.)

A mixture with an Armenian Pentecostal movement took place in 1906. A group migrating from Russia in the last part of the nineteenth century found its way to California and came into contact with the Azusa mission. Pentecostals have been called the "third force of Christendom." Within seventy years they have grown until they claim a membership of eight and a half million members.

A neo-Pentecostalism has arisen in the United States in the last ten years. Its origin has been traced to St. Mark's Episcopal Church in Van Nuys, California. The Rector Dennis Bennett first became involved in glossolalia. It then spread to the members of the church where he preached. It was at first bitterly opposed by the Episcopal religious authorities, but it spread like wildfire. In ten years, it has touched nearly every religious group in the United States.

One of the chief means of the spreading of this neo-Pentecostalism has been the Full Gospel Business Men's Fellowship International—FGBMFI. Oral Roberts helped at its organization in Los Angeles in 1960. Now there are chapters throughout the United States and in many parts of the world. Three of their magazines are Voice, Trinity and Testimony. Advocates of this neo-Pentecostalism include business executives, movie stars, T. V. personalities and college professors. (Glossolalia, by Jimmy Jividen, pp. 73-74.)

1. Through the instrumentality of the Holy Spirit, miracles of healing incurable diseases occurs today, as well as other notable miracles such as characterized the apostolic church of the first century.

p. 25, A. B. Simpson, The Gospel of Healing and E. E. Bynum in Divine Healing, p. 36.

1. Jesus advised the sick to call for a doctor. Matthew 9:12.

2. The same men who were to heal the sick in Jesus' name could also drink deadly poison, take up serpents, raise the dead, etc., which things they did in the first century in fulfillment of His promise. Mark 16:17-20.

3. Jesus spoke God's word and confirmed it with signs. Hebrews 2:3-4.

4. Miracles were performed for the purpose of confirming new truths delivered to the saints, and to produce faith. John 20:30-31.

5. Now, faith comes by hearing the word of God. Romans 10:17.

6. The fact that all truths of the gospel were "once and for all delivered" (Jude 3), proves there is no purpose that signs continue.

7. Natural healing today is Divine, but no miraculous (contrary to or apart from God's natural laws), visible, instantaneous cures are occurring today. "Every good gift and every perfect gift is from above. James 1:17.

2. A person may speak in tongues today while under the influence of the Holy Spirit, just as did Peter and the other apostles on the day of Pentecost, A.D. 33.

Cf. Pentecostalism's magazines: Truth, Voice, and Testimony, and other writings.

1. Three representative supernatural gifts are listed in 1 Corinthians 13 : 8 - 10. Tongues is one of them. Paul by inspiration of the Holy Spirit wrote they would "cease" when "that which is perfect is come." At the time of this writing, all truths of the "perfect law of liberty," the New Covenant of Jesus Christ, had not been fully revealed unto men. See James 1:25.

2. Compare Ephesians 4:8-16. Gifts were given unto men "till" the completeness of Christ's doctrine and spiritual knowledge was made known to the apostles. The gifts c e a s e d, including tongues, when the fulness of the gospel was revealed by the time John laid down his pen of inspiration in A.D. 90 in completing the book of Revelation.

3. "Tongues" were for unbelievers, not believers. 1 Corinthians 14:22.

3. Pentecostalism espouses religion as a "romantic" philosophy—that "the heart of man has reasons which his mind knows not of" (in making decisions on religious questions). Truth is

1. The Bible is truth. John 17:17. The truth is not subjective, that is, does not originate with a person's own thinking.

2. The Bible must be studied and obeyed. 2 Timothy

subjective; that is, it is not something which has objective reality, but is changed or even comes into existence by the mental s t a t e s of thinking minds. Man's feelings are the highest authority.

2:15; John 8:32.

3. The Bible is the absolute, inspired and authoritative Word of God. 2 Timothy 3:16-17; 2 Peter 1:20-21; 1 Corinthians 2:9-13.

4. When a man comes to regard his _feelings_ as the basic authority, he is on the downward path to Pentecostalism. To reject the Word of God and do "that which is right in our own eyes" is to reject God. 1 Samuel 15:22-26; Matthew 7:13-14.

4. Women may participate in leading in public prayer, teaching and preaching.
  —Commonly practiced.

1. The Holy Spirit contrasted the duties of men from that of women in public prayer. 1 Timothy 2:8-15.

2. Women are to learn in silence. 1 Corinthians 14:34. They are not to teach in any capacity over a man.

3. Woman may teach younger women. Titus 2:4. They may teach a man in private. Acts 18:25.

4. Women may not "teach" (deliver didactic discourses), hence are forbidden to preach. 1 Corinthians 14: 34.

Fuller study given in:
  a. Spiritual Sword, October 1972, article by James Meadows.

b. Roy H. Lanier, Sr., May Women Lead Prayer in Worship? Firm Foundation, Austin, Texas, 1966, p. 713.

c. Women's Limitations In Worship, by Joe D. Schubert. Star Bible Publications, 16 pp.

5. Holy Spirit baptism is for today.

1. Jesus promised the apostles would receive the baptism in the Holy Spirit, which promise was fulfilled. Acts 1:8; Acts 2:1-4.

2. There was only one other recorded case of Holy Spirit baptism like what happened on Pentecost. Acts 10; 11: 15.

3. Jesus charged his disciples to teach and baptize believers "unto the end of the world" (Mark 16 : 15 - 16; Matthew 28:18-20). Baptism in water is the only baptism that can be commanded, because men can obey it alone. Holy Spirit baptism was never a command, but a promise for certain people for special purposes.

4. Near the end of the New Testament, when Paul wrote "there is one baptism," Ephesians 4:5, Peter wrote baptism is in water, 1 Peter 3:21. Water baptism, not

Holy Spirit baptism, is "unto the end of the world."

5. "The gift of the Holy Spirit" is given when a believer is baptized in water into Christ, but this must not be confused with baptism in the Holy Spirit. Acts 2:38; Acts 5:32.

6. Instruments of music are used to "glorify" God in worship.

1. True worship is according to "Spirit and truth." John 4:24.

2. The words of Christ (not Moses, not our own feelings, emotions, and preferences) shall judge us in the Last Day. John 12:48.

3. Vocal music was repeatedly specified as the kind enjoined in Christians' worship. See Colossians 3:16; Ephesians 5:19.

4. Christians "abide in the teachings of Christ." 2 John 9-10.

5. Christians follow the pattern given by God, Hebrews 8:5, without adding, subtracting or altering according to our own desires or opinions.

7. Healing is the atonement. Christ redeemed us "from the curse of the law," and sickness is the curse of the law, destroyed by Christ.

1. The Christian is not promised release from sicknesses, but grace to endure them. 2 Corinthians 12:9.

Oral Roberts, _If You Need Healing—Do These Things_, pp. 25-26.

"Is Divine Healing In The Atonement? We believe it is . . . Through the Fall we lost everything. Jesus recovered all through His atonement . . . we are redeemed from the entire curse, body, soul, and spirit."

F. F. Bosworth, _Christ The Healer_, p. 25, 38.

Physical as well as spiritual losses were sustained through Adam's rebellion, and Christ regained all that was lost through Adam.

Mrs. Beulah Bucklen, 59, of Charleston, W. Va., died last night, eight days after being bitten twice by a rattlesnake in a snake-handling ritual at Jesus Pentecostal Church at Frazier's Bottom in Putman County, near Charleston. Roscoe Bucklen, her husband, said he persuaded her to seek medical attention when she became violently ill the day after being bitten. Bucklen, who was sitting in his car ourside the church when his wife was bitten, said: "I've seen that snake before. It's as big around as your arm. It hit her twice between the thumb and forefinger on the left hand. They had to pull the fangs from her."

2. Paul gloried gladly in his infirmity ("astheneia" is the most common Greek word for sickness). 2 Corinthians 12:9-10.

3. Many afflictions were endured by Paul for the sake of Christ. 2 Corinthians 11:23-27. Who could say Paul was not spiritually saved, delivered out of the power of darkness? Colossians 1:13-14.

4. Christ said Paul was chosen to preach the gospel to Gentiles, but was also called to "suffer for my name's sake." Acts 9:15-16.

5. Peter suffered for Christ and rejoiced that he had the privilege. Acts 5:41-42. 1 Peter 4:16.

6. Although God is interested in His children's welfare and will supply all his needs to endure affliction, Psalms 34:15-19 reads: "The eyes of the Lord are upon the righteous, and his ears are open unto their cry."

7. Paul left Trophimus "at Miletus sick." 2 Timothy 4:20. Was this saint really unsaved? All physical sickness is a part of the process of dying, which has come as a consequence of Adam's transgression and which was

Newspaper reports such as this are common, verifying the truth that miracles and signs have ceased (1 Corinthians 13) and that sincere persons may believe lies, but nevertheless must pay the consequences. This is proof that Mark 16:17-18 does not apply today, despite the empty claims of m o d e r n pseudo-miracle workers.

(Ft. Worth Star Telegram Sept. 25, 1972) 20-C

not changed by Calvary. Death for the Christian is viewed as a precious event in the sight of God. Philippians 1:21-23.

Chapter Thirteen

ARMSTRONGISM

Brief History:

The Worldwide Church of God (formerly the Radio Church of God) meets throughout the USA and in several foreign countries behind unlabeled doors in rented halls every Saturday.

Few cults are flourishing more than Armstrongism. Ambassador College Press was publishing 1,610,000 copies of "Plain Truth" magazine in 1969, in addition to the newer "Tomorrow's World" magazine. "The World Tomorrow" is regularly heard on more than 300 stations, and its television log is rapidly growing . . . reaching all of the USA plus Canada, Asia, Europe, and Latin America. On these programs, never a prayer is offered and never a hymn is sung. The true and basic tenets of the sect are concealed while popular and excellent teaching on morals, pollution, drug abuse, etc. are abundantly expounded. People who write in to the Pasadena address are contacted by Armstrongite ministers (not listed in phone books as such) and many are becoming affiliated with the Worldwide Church of God—other thousands who would never dream of leaving their own church read the printed material and send in money.

The origin and basic beliefs of Armstrongism are revealed in Herbert W. Armstrong's book, <u>The United States and British</u>

Commonwealth in Prophecy. Here, the "key" to the understanding of the Bible is said to be the identification of the United States and Great Britain in prophecy . . . a doctrine first taught by Richard Brothers (1757-1854) in England, and later clearly stated by John Wilson in Our Israelitist Origin written in 1840. The movement started when Mrs. Herbert W. Armstrong claimed that an angel revealed God's will to her. She shared her revelation with her husband who became the prophet of the movement. Herbert W. Armstrong began to preach Anglo-Israelism in 1934 in Eugene, Oregon, but did not publish his basic text (The United States and British Commonwealth in Prophecy) until 1967.

NOTE: The author gratefully acknowledges valuable assistance from Roger R. Chambers, minister, West Side Church of Christ, Hamilton, Ohio, who spent two years of intensive research on the subject while studying for his Master's Degree at Cincinnati Bible College. His work has been published under the title, The Plain Truth About Armstrongism, 144 pages ($1.25, paper).

ARMSTRONG TRADITION	WORD OF GOD
1. Mrs. Herbert W. Armstrong received revelations from an angel of the way of God. Chambers, Plain Truth About Armstrongism, p. 9.	1. Galatians 1:8-9: no man or angel to speak differently from New Testament without being anathema.
2. Herbert W. Armstrong affirms his ministry is from heaven, and that the gospel was not preached "for eighteen and one half centuries." (Plain Truth About Armstrongism, 15). H. W. Armstrong, The Inside Story of the World Tomorrow Broadcast, p. 7-11.	1. Jesus' gospel and His words shall never pass away. The Bible has never been destroyed by men in any age or time.
"By God's direction and authority, I have laid the truth before you." H. W. Armstrong, The United States and British Commonwealth in Prophecy, p. 212.	2. The word of God, once given. Jude 3; John 17:17.
All the rest of the world in "total ignorance." Ibid., p. 6 (Plain Truth About Armstrongism, 16).	Armstrong revealed what God concealed! Christians have concealed that which God did reveal (the gospel).
3. "Lost Israel" is to be identified as the Anglo-Saxon peoples, the key to understanding the Bible. Plain Truth About Armstrongism, 18.	1. Term "lost tribes of Israel" not in Bible.
[Garner Ted Armstrong and his father both disavow any connection with or	2. All liars will have their place.

knowledge of British Israelism, but the book The United States and British Commonwealth in Prophecy has the doctrine in it throughout, though not labeled "British-I s r a e l i s m" or "Anglo-Israelism."]

[If Armstrong admitted his "key" doctrine was preached by British-Israelites before he did, then obviously he received no revelation from heaven but merely read books on the subject and re-vamped their doctrines. Read Armstrong's book The United States and British Commonwealth in Prophecy, then read one of the standard British-Israel texts such as J. H. Allen's Judah's Sceptre and Joseph's Birthright first written in 1902. Except for the Sabbath doctrine and Armstrong's modern predictions, you will be reading the same doctrine.]

Plain Truth About Armstrongism, p. 19-22.

4. The old British-Israel theory has the deathbed promises of Jacob favoring the younger son, Ephraim, instead of Manasseh, who was to become a lesser nation. When Britian flourished, it was fashionable to apply Ephraim to that great nation and to assert the throne of David is the throne in England where God's people would be ruled over until Christ's return when he will

1. Genesis 48 makes no mention of what nations specifically would arise in fulfillment of Jacob's promises and blessings.

take over and reign in victory.

However, w h e n Armstrong saw the nation of England on the wane as compared with the United States (Manasseh), he reversed the interpretation so as to give the favored blessing to the United States!

Plain Truth About Armstrongism, pp. 21-24.

5. The theory of the "Lost Ten Tribes" calls for (1) all inhabitants of the northern kingdom of Hoshea to be deported by Shalmaneser and Sargon, 722-718 B.C.; (2) The House of Israel has never returned but has remained intact somewhere as a people—a total population in anonymous pilgrimage.

Plain Truth About Armstrongism, 25-26.

Armstrong claims this ancient m y s t e r y is now "cleared up" by him.

Plain Truth About Armstrongism, 34-35.

[Over two dozen lost tribes hunters have made such assertions, including the Mormons who say it is the Lamanites—ancestors of American Indians.]

The house of Israel (nor-

1. Many deportations t o many lands of Hebrew people resulted from various wars. Numbers 31:35; Amos 1:9; 1 Kings 20:34; Jeremiah 52:28-30.

Plain Truth About Armstrongism, 37-39.

2. Proselyting also disseminated Israelite culture. Isaiah 14:1; 66:21; Matthew 23:15, Pharisees compassed land and sea; Esther 8:17, "many people b e c a m e Jews," Ruth and Rahab; Isaiah 56:3, J u d a i z e d "strangers."

3. Women have been abused in wars and by armies and the children of such victims among Hebrew women were raised Jewish, though racially they were a mixed race. Deuteronomy 28:30; Exodus 15:9; Judges 5:30; Isa-

thern tribes) was lost then found removed to the British Isles.

iah 13:16. The Jews of Germany are the descendants of beautiful Jewish women of Austria, who were taken prisoners and raped by the Vangioni; these women raised their children in the Jewish religion. (H. Graetz, History of the Jews, III, p. 40f).

Plain Truth About Armstrongism, 44-5.

4. Deportations were not total populations, but only a few of the e l i t e, the governors, the wealthy, the political leaders, etc. Jeremiah 52:27-30; 2 Kings 24: 14-16. The masses of common people were never removed after any war.

Plain Truth About Armstrongism, 55-57.

Name "Jew" is used 174 times in the New Testament, but name "Israel" is used 75 times. Jesus identified the house of Israel with the Jews in Palestine of his day. Matthew 10:5-6, go to the lost sheep of house of Israel. (inhabitants of Judea). See Jeremiah 50:17; Matthew 15:24-26.

6. The hope of Israel is national, racial, geographic.

1. Acts 26:6-7:The hope of Israel involves the claim of

Armstrong, The United States and British Commonwealth in Prophecy.

Christ and spiritual values and benefits. Acts 28:20; John 18:36.

2. The land promise was fulfilled. Exodus 23:30-31; Deuteronomy 1:8; Joshua 21:19 43, 45; Nehemiah 9:7-8.

3. Acts 1:6: "Dost thou at this time restore the kingdom to Israel?"

[If "literal," then Israelite race must be available for political reconstitution; if spiritual, then existence of 'lost tribes' is of no consequence.]

4. Ephesians 2:12-15: distinction of Jew and Gentile is lost in Christ. Galatians 3:28.

7. "Jesus Christ will not sit upon the throne of David until His second coming, yet future."

The United States and British Commonwealth in Prophecy, p. 69.

1. The kingdom of God promised to both Israel and Judah is the church, and Christ as head is now reigning over it upon the throne of David. Acts 2:29-33; Acts 15:14-17; Amos 9:11-12; Romans 10:11-13; Acts 13:30-34. Jesus now reigns. Revelation 2:25-27; 1 Corinthians 15:24-28.

8. Prophecies of Old Testament for the 20th Century primarily.

The United States and

1. Acts 3:24.
2. Acts 26:22-23.
3. Daniel 7:13-14. Jesus went to God in heaven to

ARMSTRONG TRADITION	WORD OF GOD
British Commonwealth in Prophecy, p. 132.	receive His Kingdom. Acts 1:9. 4. Luke 24:44-48. The main body of prophecy focused upon Jesus' death, burial, resurrection and the preaching of the gospel. Isaiah 2:2-4.
9. The Sabbath and the Law still binding . . . the Ten Commandments the way to salvation. The United States and British Commonwealth in Prophecy, p. 161.	1. See passages under study on Seventh Day Adventism. 2 Corinthians 3:4-14; Colossians 2:13-17.

The
New Testament
Church

By
L. R. WILSON

The New Testament Church
ITS BEGINNING

The church described by the New Testament rests upon seven cardinal principles. These are: (1) the death of Christ; (2) the resurrection of Christ; (3) the ascension of Christ; (4) the sending of the Holy Spirit by Christ; (5) baptism by His authority; (6) baptism "into the name of the Father and of the Son and the Holy Spirit"; and (7) salvation in the name of Christ. Apart from these foundation stones there could be no *New Testament Church*.

There could be no New Testament church until these foundation stones were all firmly laid. When and where were these first laid?

Some six months before the death of our Lord, He said: "Upon this rock I will build my church" (Matthew 16:18). At that time the building of our Lord's church was still in the future. But from the first Pentecost following His resurrection the church was always spoken of as something in existence, and people were being "added to it" (Acts 2:47). It follows then that the church had its beginning between the time Jesus promised to build it and the close of the next Pentecost day.

In the second chapter of Acts for the first time was made the announcement of all the seven cardinal facts upon which the church rests. Speaking by the Holy Spirit, the apostle Peter publicly declared that Jesus had been "delivered up by the determinate council and foreknowledge of God," and that "by the hands of lawless men" He had been crucified and slain, whom "God raised up, whereof we are all witnesses." He then explained: "Being therefore by the right hand of God exalted, and having received of the Father the promise of the Holy Spirit, he hath poured forth this which you now see and hear" — the outpouring of the Holy Spirit.

Those who heard the words of the apostle were pricked in their hearts, and cried out, "Brethren, what shall we do? And Peter said unto them, Repent ye, and be baptized everyone of you in the name of Jesus Christ unto the remission of your sins; and ye shall receive the gift of the Holy Spirit" (Acts 2:32-38).

Acting under the Great Commission (Matthew 28:19-20) which the apostles had received of the Lord to go and "make disciples of all nations, baptizing them into the name of the Father and of the Son and of the Holy Spirit" the apostle Peter thus announced for the first time baptism by the authority of the Lord Jesus Christ, and "into the name of the Father and of the Son and the Holy Spirit."

Thus, baptism was first proclaimed by Christ's authority on this day. It was administered — according to the Great Commission of Christ — "into the name" of God; and remission of sins, or salvation, was proclaimed in HIS NAME on this day for the first time (Luke 24:46-47). A few days later Peter explained, "And in none other is there salvation: for neither is there any other name under heaven that is given among men, wherein we must be saved" (Acts 4:12).

Since all of the foundation stones upon which the church rests were firmly planted upon the first Pentecost following the resurrection of our Lord — in the city of Jerusalem — the church was henceforth spoken of as being in existence. Indeed, the apostle Peter actually spoke of this day as "the beginning" (Acts 11:15). Jesus also spoke of it as the beginning date for the proclamation of the Gospel of Christ. Thus the laws governing His church became functional on the very day it was started, and all men from then until now enter it the same way.

We do not, therefore, go back before the death of Christ upon the cross to learn the terms of entrance into His church, or kingdom. We do not go back to the law of Moses to learn how to worship God in the church set forth in the New Testament. Neither do we look forward to Christ's return for the establishment of His reign upon this earth. He is our King now. We are His subjects now. We are amenable to all of His laws now. When He comes again it will not be to set up a kingdom, but to raise all that are in the graves, either to "the resurrection of life" or to "the resurrection of condemnation" (John 5:28)

Any church that did not start in the City of Jerusalem, on the first Pentecost following the resurrection of our Lord, is not His. Any system not found in the New Testament constitutes no part of the church therein set forth, or the principles governing it.

All that we know about the church of our Lord, or the principles by which it is governed, we learn from the New Testament, and it alone. ★

The New Testament Church
ITS CREED

The church set forth in the New Testament has a creed, but not of human origin. Our confession is not in a set of rules and dogmas, but in the Divine Sonship of the Lord Jesus Christ. Indeed, OUR CREED IS CHRIST.

We believe that Jesus was a good man, a great teacher, a great philosopher, a great leader and a great ruler. But our belief in Him goes much further. We might believe all of these facts and still be rank infidels. In fact, nearly all infidels do believe in Jesus to this extent. But we believe in Jesus as "the Christ, the Son of the living God." It is upon the confession of this great truth that the church of our Lord Jesus Christ rests (Matthew 16:16-19).

This is the confession made by God the Father when Jesus was baptized (Matthew 3:16-17), and again at the time of His transfiguration (Matthew 17:5). It is the same confession made by Jesus Himself which cost Him His earthly life (Matthew 26:63-64; Mark 14:60-65). It is the confession made by the Ethiopian officer (Acts 8:36-38). It is the same confession made by all the early Christians (Romans 10:9-10; Ephesians 3:14).

Belief in Jesus Christ as the Son of the living God means belief that He is Divine; that He is God incarnate. It means that He was; and is perfect in all His ways — a perfect teacher, a perfect philosopher, a perfect propitiation of our sins. It means that He is our King Supreme. In His nature and character, in His wisdom and righteousness, in His authority and power, and in His decisions and judgment.

We also believe the Bible, not merely because of its antiquity, or some tradition which has grown up around it but because it is a revelation of the mind of God.

We do not go to the Old Testament to learn how to become Christians. But from the Old Testament we do learn of God's dealings with His people in ages past, His regard for man, for truth and uprightness. From it we can learn to respect God's judgment, what it means to obey or disobey His commands, and the consequences of our obedience or our disobedience to His will.

But if we want to know how to enter the kingdom of God today, how to become God's children, how to worship Him in our public assemblies, how to conduct ourselves as His children at this present time, then we turn to the New Testament.

We do not believe in baptism because of any special merit that it carries. We do not believe in partaking of the Lord's supper because of any inherent good which we derive from it. We do not believe in prayer solely because of its psychological value to ourselves. First of all, we believe in Jesus Christ as the Son of the living God. In accepting Him as such we must accept His teachings, His authority, His judgments and His absolute right to direct all of our ways. We cannot substitute our own reasoning, our own desires for absolute belief in Christ as God's Son and for His authority.

Upon this ground and it alone all all believers in Christ be united. All of the angels and archangels might assemble in council for eons but never could they draw up a constitution for the church of the living God. With the followers of Jesus Christ scattered over the face of the whole earth, all with their own peculiar bits of reasoning, likes and dislikes, they could never be united on any human creed, any set of dogmas, or under any earthly authority. God very well knew this long before the church was established. Hence He gave us a living creed centered in the Divinity of the living Christ who was raised from the dead to die no more. He is the Alpha and the Omega, the beginning and the end. By faith in Him alone can we all unite as a mighty army, against one common enemy — the force of evil — and with one common goal, the ultimate triumph over the powers of darkness, and an entrance into the eternal Paradise of God, where evil, desputings, parties, strife, and warring factions have no place.

*

The New Testament Church
ITS TERMS OF DESIGNATION

The church set forth in the New Testament is described by a number of different pictures. Since it is a spiritual institution, and different from anything else in existence, it could not be adequately represented by any one figure or picture.

The original term for "church" signifies a "called out" body of people. All who are in it have been called out from a state of sin, from the world, from the kingdom of darkness, or from a state of "death" (Ephesians 2:5). They have been called into the kingdom of God's dear Son (Colossians 1:13), frequently spoken of as "the kingdom of heaven" (Matthew 3:2), or the kingdom of God (Luke 10:9-11).

Often this divine institution, generally referred to in the New Testament as the "church," carries no particular designation, other than that of its location. Thus we read of the church at Corinth, at Colossae, at Ephesus, etc.

If we think of this divine institution as a called out body of people over whom Christ reigns as head and in which the Holy Spirit dwells, then it is the body of Christ (Colossians 1:18; Ephesians 1:20-22). If we think of God as the Father of us all, and ourselves as brethren, and joint-heirs with Christ Jesus (Romans 8:16-17), then we constitute the family, or "the house of God, which is the church of the living God, the pillar and the ground of the truth" (1 Timothy 3:15).

If we think of this same body with Christ ruling over it as our King, with the whole world as its territory, with the New Testament as its constitution, then it is the kingdom of God, or of "His dear Son." Jesus referred to the church and the kingdom in one and the same breath, thus signifying the same institution (Matthew 16:18-19). If we think of it as a kingdom, then it is the kingdom of God, the kingdom of Christ, or the kingdom of heaven. They are all one and the same. Jesus could say, "All things that are mine" (John 17:10). This divine institution is spoken of as the kingdom of heaven, because it is heaven-born and it was purchased with the blood of the Lord Jesus Christ, who came down from heaven.

The church is frequently called "the church of God;" sometimes "the church of the living God;" "the church of the Firstborn"

(Hebrews 12:23). Once Jesus merely spoke of it as "my church" (Matthew 16:18). When various congregations were spoken of in the plural they were sometimes called "the churches of Christ (Romans 16:16).

Whether we refer to a single congregation, or to the whole body of Christ, they may rightfully be referred to as HIS. In order "that in all things he might have the preeminence" (Colossians 1:18), we usually speak of it as Christ's church, or the church of Christ. This in no way detracts from the many references in which it is spoken of as the church of God, or kingdom of God; nor does it in any way make it a sect or denomination.

The church in the New Testament was not referred to as just another religious body among many. It was something altogether new and different from anything that had ever existed before. When Jesus said, "upon this rock I will build my church" (Matthew 16:18), He was alluding to all of His followers, or all of God's people.

When the term "church" was used with respect to God's people in Ephesus, Corinth, Philippi, and other places, then it included all of God's people in that particular location. The individuals who made up the family of God were spoken of as disciples, followers of Christ, brethren, children of God, Christians, fellow-workers, servants, or by some other single term which characterized their relationship to God, to Christ or to one another.

At no time was the church ever used as an adjective. We never find such terms as "a Church of Christ preacher," "a Church of God member," or "a Church of the Lord elder." Such phraseology would have been misleading. It is no less so today. Neither do we ever find the church referred to by such expressions which characterize the MEMBERS of the body of Christ. It is never called "the Disciples Church," "the Church of the Brethren," or "the Christian Church." Such terms would have implied that God recognized a plurality of sectarian bodies which was never the case. It ought not so to be today.

Let us be careful that we never "denominationalize" the church of our Lord. All such sectarian terms are what have contributed to the large number of denominations today. And denominational bodies divide the people of God. This is contrary to Christ's prayer for unity (John 17:20-23).   ★

The New Testament Church
ITS NATURE

Jesus did not come into the world to establish an earthly government. There is no reference or allusion to the church as if it were "a new society" — meaning a society or institution that functions as a world government, with all of the powers of both a worldly and ecclesiastical body. It has no temporal power or earthly functions whatsoever. Jesus declared, "My kingdom is not of this world" (John 18:36). His kingdom's boundaries are that of truth and righteousness, purity and holiness.

Christ's church is described by many images in order to convey some concept of its divine nature. Sometimes it is described as God's "building" (Ephesians 2:19-22; 1 Peter 2:5). Sometimes it is pictured as Christ's body. Paul said "Now ye are the body of Christ, and severally members thereof" (1 Corinthians 12:27; see also Ephesians 1:20-23; Colossians 1:18).

The church also is pictured as a kingdom. Sometimes it is spoken of as "the kingdom of God" (Matthew 6:33; Mark 1:14); "the kingdom of His dear Son" (Colossians 1:13); or, more frequently, it is represented as "the kingdom of heaven" (Matthew 3:2; 7:21; 16:19).

This divine institution is entered by a new birth — "of water and of the spirit" (John 3:5). It is not possible to enter it in any other way. However, before one is "born again . . . of water and of the spirit" it is necessary to believe in Jesus Christ as the only begotten Son of God, to turn one's back upon all past sins, to publicly acknowledge the name of Christ, at which time one becomes a proper subject for a burial in water "in order to the remission of sins" (Romans 6:3-4; Acts 2:38). Thus, one is "born again", or as the term is sometimes rendered, "born anew" or "born from above." All of these terms mean conversion.

The blessings of the church are of a spiritual nature. One may never attend church at all, yet if he is an honorable and upright man in all of his dealings, he may enjoy the same MATERIAL blessings that the most devout Christian enjoys. But he cannot know "the peace of God, which passeth all understanding" (Philippians 4:7).

Paul declared that God "hath blessed us with every spiritual blessing in the heavenly places IN CHRIST JESUS" (Ephesians 1:3).

To be in Christ is to be in His spiritual body, which is His church. In it, therefore, we enjoy "every spiritual blessing." There are NO SPIRITUAL BLESSINGS outside of Christ, or His church.

Paul further declared that all of the promises of God are in Christ Jesus (1 Corinthians 1:20). In Christ we have salvation (2 Timothy 2:10). In Him "we have redemption through his blood, the forgiveness" (Ephesians 1:7).

Thus, the church is composed of men and women (Romans 12:5; 1 Corinthians 12:27); but not just any and every kind. All who are in the kingdom have been born again (John 3:3,5); they have been called out from the world (for so is the meaning of the term church); they have become new creatures in Christ Jesus (2 Corinthians 5:17). All such can say with Paul, "I am crucified with Christ; nevertheless I live; yet not I, but Christ liveth in Me" (Galatians 2:20).

Being a spiritual institution, the church of our Lord was not founded for the natural man. It was founded for the spirit of man, that part that lives forever. Hence, the church will not pass away with the death of our bodies. It was built to stand "forever." The gates of Hades can never destroy it (Matthew 16:18). Its purpose is to prepare man to dwell with God forever.

All civic organizations, all of the lodges of men, and all human institutions of every kind were founded for the natural man; that part of man that will finally die and return to the earth from whence it came. But the church of the Lord, being a heavenly institution, was founded for the spirit, or soul of man, that part that never dies. Human institutions may comfort us during our life on earth. But beyond the grave they cannot go. They were not built to stand forever. They must all pass away with time. But the church built by our Lord can and will conduct our souls into the everlasting Paradise of God, to dwell with Him throughout all eternity. *

The New Testament Church
ITS ORGANIZATION

In structure the New Testament church has the most simple organization conceivable, yet the strongest and most durable. Civilizations have come and gone, kingdoms have risen and fallen, social orders have flourished and vanished, but the church of our Lord still endures. Truly, "the gates of Hades shall not prevail against it" (Matthew 16:18). The greatest weakness in the institutions of men are often their top-heavy organizations. In their efforts to become strong they often become weak.

The church set forth in the New Testament has a divine head. Christ is that head (Colossians 1:18). He became head of His church after His resurrection from the dead (Ephesians 1:20-23). When Christ was raised from the dead it was to die no more, "death hath no more dominion over him" (Romans 6:8-10). He has never relinquished His headship to anyone. He has never surrendered His authority to another. To John He said, I am he that liveth and was dead; and, behold I am alive for evermore" (Revelation 1:18). He has no vicar on earth; no one rules in His stead. The church of the New Testament, being a spiritual institution, and "not of this world," has no earthly head.

The church of our Lord had the apostles to direct it in the beginning. These were specifically chosen by Christ Himself and specially endowed for a PARTICULAR work they were given to do. Before they were sent forth to perform their mission Christ carefully taught them for a period of some three years, then after His departure He sent forth the Holy Spirit to guide them in all that they taught (John 16:13).

As an evidence of His approval, and that the Holy Spirit was with them, the apostles were enabled to speak in other tongues, perform miracles, and to withstand all the accusations of their enemies, while confounding them with the evidences which the Lord has promised to them (Mark 13:10-11; 16:18-20; Acts 2:1-4; Hebrews 2:4). The work of the apostles was such that they could have no successors in office. It is evident that the work given to them to perform needs no revision; we can never add to or take from what they wrote, or what they did (Galatians 1:8-9; Jude 3; Revelations 22:18-19).

In New Testament times each congregation had a plurality of elders (Acts 14:23). These same men were also called bishops or "overseers" of the church (Acts 20:17-28). Their duties were to oversee the congregation and serve as pastors or shepherds to those committed to their care. Paul and Peter, himself also an elder, concur in what they taught about the duties of elders (Acts 20:28-29; 1 Peter 5:1-3).

The only officers were those who served a local congregation. Each congregation had elders, who served the particular congregation, and it alone.

Each congregation had a plurality of deacons. The first of these are mentioned in Acts 6:1-6. They are mentioned again, along with the bishops in the church at Philippi (Philippians 1:1). Their qualifications are set forth in 1 Timothy 3:8-10.

The deacons were chosen to perform special duties or services assigned to them by the elders. The word deacons always carries the idea of servant.

There is a sense in which all of God's children are servants. But deacons were especially chosen and assigned to perform particular services. This was characteristic of each congregation when it was sufficiently established.

The evangelists of the early church were to primarily "preach the word" (2 Timothy 4:2). An evangelist might serve as a deacon, as an elder, or as a teacher, but the word "evangelist" carries the idea of a bearer of good news. This was his first and foremost duty.

There were no other officers in the early church. If these were sufficient then, they should be sufficient to govern the church of God today. And, indeed, they are. ★

The New Testament Church
ITS DAY OF WORSHIP

Jesus was raised from the dead on the first day of the week. In the language of Paul, He was thus "declared to be the Son of God with power . . . by the resurrection from the dead" (Romans 1:4). It was on this day that He first appeared to His disciples. One week later He appeared to them again — on the first day of the week.

The church was begun on the day of Pentecost, which also fell on the first day of the week — fifty days after the feast of the passover which ended with the Sabbath (Leviticus 23:15-16).

The seventh day Sabbath was given to the Jews in commemoration of their deliverance from Egyptian bondage (Deuteronomy 5:15). But the resurrection of our Lord signified our deliverance from sin and the grave.

It was fitting therefore, that the church should have its beginning on the first day of the week, and that thereafter Christians should assemble on this day for the express purpose of worshipping God in commemorating the sufferings and death of the Lord Jesus Christ in the observance of the Lord's Supper.

Though we sometimes find Paul going into the Jewish synagogues in different cities on the Jewish Sabbath, he did so for the express purpose of preaching the Gospel to the Jews, persuading them to give up their former manner of worship and turn to the Lord Jesus Christ. As for Christians, in the New Testament, we never find them meeting for the express purpose of worshipping on the Jewish Sabbath, but always on the first day of the week; "And upon the first day of the week, when the disciples came together TO BREAK BREAD, Paul preached unto them, ready to depart on the morrow" (Acts 20:7). While the early Christians engaged in other acts of worship when they came together at their set time ("upon the first day of the week"), the apostle Paul specifically states that the PURPOSE of such meetings was "to break bread."

If it be argued that the early Christians did not necessarily meet the first day of "EVERY week" we have only to recall that in giving of the Decalogue the Israelites were merely told to "Remember the sabbath day, to keep it holy" (Exodus 20:8). One man in the camp it seems, felt that because the Lord did not specify, "EVERY Sabbath

137

day," that he might not have to keep each and every one. But when he violated just one sabbath by going out and gathering up sticks he was stoned.

We simply look to 1 Corinthians 16:1-2, where we learn that the early church met upon the first day of every week, at which time they were to make their contribution for the work the Lord had laid upon the church. "Now concerning the collection for the saints, as I have given orders to the churches of Galatia, even so do ye. Upon the first day of the week let every one of you lay by him in store, as God has prospered him, that there be no gatherings (collections) when I come." Many translations read: "Upon the first day of EVERY week," which is precisely what the original language here signifies.

Never is the first day of the week referred to in the New Testament as the "Christian Sabbath." Indeed, it is never spoken of as the "Sabbath" or even alluded to in this manner in a single instance. Furthermore, all references to the stated occasions for Christian worship indicate that it was done on "the first day of the week," but never on the seventh day, or the Jewish Sabbath. With the death of Christ the Sabbath day, which was given to the Jews in commemoration of their deliverance from Egyptian bondage, lost its meaning. In truth, it never had any significance whatsoever for Christians (Colossians 2:14-16).

Although Christians do not observe the first day of the week in the same manner that the Jews observed their Sabbath, yet because of its significance, all Christians should be faithful in their meetings upon this day to worship God to commemorate the sufferings and death of our Lord, while looking forward to His coming again. ✶

138

The New Testament Church
ITS MUSIC IN WORSHIP

That the early Christians had music in their assemblies for worship goes without saying. Indeed, they had the very best. It was vocal music accompanied only BY THE HEART. There were no mechanical instruments to mar the beautiful melody of the early saints. Mechanical instruments were first used in church about 700 years after Christ.

When God's people sing praises to Him today in their assemblies for worship they are carrying out the orders of the Holy Spirit. There is never any question about this. Christians need not apologize for, nor explain why, they worship God "in psalms and hymns and spiritual songs, singing and making melody in your heart to the Lord" (Ephesians 5:19). This is exactly what the apostle Paul, guided by the Holy Spirit, enjoined upon all Christians. And again: "Let the word of Christ dwell in you richly in all wisdom; teaching and admonishing one another in psalms and hymns and spiritual songs, singing with grace in your heart to the Lord" (Colossians 3:16).

If the Lord had wanted us to have ice cream and cake on the Lord's table He would have told us so. In like manner, if He had wanted us to use mechanical instruments of music in our worship, He would have told us.

In our efforts to follow the Lord Jesus Christ we are not governed by what He did not forbid, but by what He has authorized. In that great Sermon on the Mount, Jesus said, "Not everyone that saith unto me, Lord, Lord, shall enter into the kingdom of heaven; but he that doeth the will of my Father which is in heaven" (Matthew 7:21). We can only know the will of the Lord from the reading of His Word. When the Lord asks us to do something, then it is His will that we do it. But if He does not, then it is presumptuous to make it a part of our worship.

The fact that the apostle Paul specifically mentioned "singing" without generalizing upon the type of music we are to make to the Lord excludes any other kind. Had we merely been told to "make music" WITHOUT ANY MENTION OF THE KIND, then we would have been at liberty to sing, to play upon an instrument, or to do both. But when the New Testament specifically mentions the kind of music we are to make, then it would be presumptive on our part to add something thereto, just as it would be presumptive to add meat to the elements on the Lord's table.

When Paul said to sing and MAKE MELODY did that imply the use of a mechanical instrument?

It is true that the original word from which this term comes does signify an accompaniment. Etymologically, the term meant to "PLUCK." It might have signified the plucking of a hair from the tail or mane of a horse, or from the head of a person, or the plucking of a flower. But we can only determine the thing that was to be plucked by the use of the term.

Since no word is used with the "pluck" the context makes it evident the thing plucked in Christian worship was not a mechanical instrument but the vocal chords, used to make melody unto the Lord. The early church thus praised God with their "lips" (Hebrews 13:15).

It is true that the early Christians sang with an accompaniment. But Paul was quite specific in naming the accompaniment. It was that of the heart (Ephesians 5:19; Colossians 3:16). The instrument that accompanies our singing in Christian worship today must likewise be the heart. If the heart is not in it, then it is not spiritual worship. Thus Paul could write: "I will sing with the spirit, and I will sing with the understanding also" (1 Corinthians 14:15).

Instruments were introduced into the worship not as an "aid" for the doing of what God commanded, but rather an excuse for our failure to carry out our Lord's divine requirement, that of "singing with grace in your hearts to the Lord." ★

The New Testament Church
ITS TERMS OF ENTRANCE

When one becomes a part of the New Testament Church he leaves his old state and enters into a new state, a new relationship with God. This relationship is sometimes pictured as an entrance "into Christ." But since the church is the (spiritual) body of Christ (Ephesians 1:20-23; Colossians 1:18), then when one enters into Christ he enters into Christ's church, His kingdom, or His body.

A number of figures are used in the New Testament to represent the change which takes place in the life of the individual when he leaves his old state of sin, and enters into a new relationship with Christ. In order to convey this change to our finite minds many striking terms are used to represent it — such as "conversion," "a new birth," "regeneration," "reconciliation," redemption."

Thus, entrance into the body of Christ differs completely from entrance into any sort of human organization. No such change takes place in the life of an individual when he joins a lodge, a sectarian body, or any sort of human society. One does not "join" the church of our Lord in the sense that he joins a lodge, a sectarian body, or any sort of a human society. We can only become united with Christ, or His church (His spiritual body), by experiencing a complete change in our nature. We must die to the old life and be raised to a new life with Christ (Romans 6:3-5). We must leave our old state and enter into a completely new relationship with God through Jesus Christ.

Jesus once said, "Except a man be born again, he cannot see the kingdom of God" (John 3:3). Again He declared, "Except ye be converted, and become as little children, ye shall not enter into the kingdom of heaven" (Matthew 18:3). The apostle Peter told unrepentant sinners to "Repent . . . and be converted that your sins may be blotted out" (Acts 3:19). The apostle Paul declared that God "saved us by the washing of regeneration, and renewing of the Holy Ghost" (Titus 3:5).

These Scriptures naturally raise the question of HOW this change, known as "conversion," or "regeneration," is brought about.

The New Testament specifically stipulates four separate steps, or acts which culminate in a complete change of heart, life, or relation and by which one is translated from the kingdom of darkness into the kingdom of light, the kingdom of God's dear Son (Colossians 1:13).

1. MAN MUST BELIEVE ON THE LORD JESUS CHRIST. Jesus said, ". . . if you believe not that I am he, ye shall die in your sins" (John 8:24). Again He said, ". . . he that believeth not shall be damned" (Mark 16:16). The apostle Paul told the Philippian jailer to "Believe on the Lord Jesus Christ, and thou shall be saved" (Acts 16:32). Belief in Christ implies complete reliance upon Christ — not upon self, or anyone else.

2. MAN MUST REPENT OF HIS SINS. Jesus said, ". . . except ye repent, ye shall all likewise perish" (Luke 13:3, 5). The apostle Peter, speaking by the Holy Spirit, commanded repentance "for the remission of sins," or "that your sins may be blotted out" (Acts 2:38; 3:19). Genuine repentance means a complete about face. It means the giving up of the practice of sin and a turning to the Lord. In repentance one dies to the practice of sin and brings his life into harmony with the life of the Lord Jesus Christ.

3. ONE MUST CONFESS THE NAME OF CHRIST. We do not confess our belief in some human creed. Instead, we acknowledge our faith in Christ as the Son of God. This is evident from such Scriptures as Matthew 10:32-33; Luke 9:26; Acts 8:37; Romans 10:9-10.

4. ONE MUST BE BAPTIZED INTO CHRIST (Romans 6:3-4; Galatians 3:27). In the Great Commission Jesus said, "He that believeth and is baptized shall be saved" (Mark 16:16). The apostle Peter commanded the Pentecostans to "Repent and be baptized every one of you in the name of Jesus Christ for the remission of sins, and ye shall receive the gift of the Holy Ghost" (Acts 2:38). Ananias told Saul to "arise, and be baptized, and wash away thy sins (Acts 22:16).

When we examine all the cases of conversion in the New Testament we find each one who was converted heard the Gospel, and having been convicted of his sins, repented and acknowledged his belief in Jesus as the Christ the Son of God, and every one was baptized.

Thus, those who did, had their sins forgiven and were then added to the church (Acts 2:47), and became the recipients of the Holy Spirit. All such were born again, they were regenerated, and became new creatures in Christ Jesus the Lord (2 Corinthians 5:17). Thus, they entered into the body of Christ, His church.   ★

BIBLIOGRAPHY

Armstrong, Herbert W. The Inside Story of the World Tomorrow Broadcast. The United States and British Commonwealth In Prophecy. Pasadena, Calif. Ambassador Press, 1967.

Book of Mormon. Copyrighted 1920 by Herber J. Grant, Trustee-in-Trust for the Church of Jesus Christ of Latter Day Saints. Salt Lake City, Utah. Originally issued by Orson Pratt in 1879.

Bosworth, F. F. Christ The Healer. F. F. Bosworth, Miami, Florida, 1948. Seventh edition.

Canright, D. N. Seventh-Day Adventism Renounced. New York, Chicago, Toronto: Fleming H. Revell Company, Third Edition, 1893.

Chambers, Roger. The Plain Truth About Armstrongism. Grand Rapids: Baker Book House, 1972.

Eddy, Mrs. Mary Baker. Science and Health with Key to the Scriptures. Boston: Trustees under the Will of Mary Baker G. Eddy.

Gibbons, James Cardinal. The Faith of Our Fathers. 83rd Edition. New York: P. J. Kenedy & Son, Printers of Holy See.

Harmon, N. B. (Book Edition) Doctrines and Discipline of the Methodist Church. Nashville. The Methodist Publishing House, 1948. 691 pp.

Hiscox, Edward T. The Standard Manual For Baptist Churches. Philadelphia: The American Baptist Publication Society, 1949.

Jennings, Alvin. Birth Control. Fort Worth, Texas. Star Bible Publications, 1961.

Jividen, Jimmy. Glossolalia: From God or Man. Star Bible Publications, Fort Worth, Texas, 1971.

Lambert, O.C. Catholicism Against Itself. Vol. I,II. Winfield, Alabama: Fair Haven Publishers, 1954. [Paperback short edition also]

Luthers Shorter Catechism. An explanation of Luther's Small Catechism, edited by Joseph Stump DD,LLD (United Lutheran Publishing House Evangelical Lutheran Church in North America)

Make Sure of All Things. Brooklyn, N. Y. Watchtower Society.

Martin and Klann. The Christian Science Myth. Grand Rapids. Zondervan, 1955.

Mead, F. S. Handbook on Denominations in the United States: Nashville: Abingdon Press. Fourth Edition.

Methodist Discipline (Episcopal South). Nashville, Tennessee: Methodist Publishing Co., 1914.

Miller, W. D. Modern Divine Healing. Miller Publishing Co., Fort Worth, Tex, 1956.

Norris, J. P. The Catechism and Prayer Book. London, Longmans, Green, & Co., 1892, 502 pp.

Pendleton, J. M. Baptist Church Manual. Philadephia: The American Baptist Society.

Pentecostal Church Manual. St. Louis: Pentecostal Publishing House.

Religious Bodies. Statistics, History and Doctrines: Washington, U. S. Department of Commerce, 1936.

Roark, W. C. compiler. Divine Healing, The Worner Press, Anderson, Ind. 1945.

Roberts, Oral. If You Need Healing—Do These Things. Standard Printing Co., Tulsa, 1949. Fifth Edition.

Rosten, Leo. A Guide To The Religions in America. New York: Simon and Schuster. 1955.

Russell, Charles T., Studies in the Scriptures (Seven Volumes). Watchtower Bible and Tract Society, Brooklyn, New York, 1891-1926.

Schaff, Philip. History of the Christian Church. Grand Rapids: Eerdmans, 1950. Vol. 1-8.

Simpson, A. B. The Gospel of Healing. Christian Alliance Publishing Co., New York, 1915.

Stump, Joseph. An explanation of Luther's Small Catechism. Philadelphia: The United Lutheran Publication House, 1935.

Thayer, J. Henry, D. D. Greek-English Lexicon on the New Testament. New York, Cincinnati, Chicago: American Book Company, 1889.

Tomlinson, L. G. Churches of Today in the Light of Scriptures. Nashville, Gospel Advocate Co., 1927.

Warren, Thomas B. The Spiritual Sword. Getwell Church of Christ, 1511 Getwell Rd., Memphis, Oct. 1972, Vol. 4, No. 1. Theme: Mysticism and Emotionalism In Religion.

Wilhite, J. Porter. Modern Churches and the Church. Oklahoma City: Telegram Book Company, 1956.

ADDITIONAL MATERIALS

1. Traditions of Men Vs. The Word of God
        By Alvin Jennings
        Single Copies   1.50
        Per Dozen   15.00
        Per 100   95.00
            (Add 10% for Postage)

2. Holy Bible
        Old and New Testaments, Maps,
        Charts and Concordance   2.75
            (Add 10% for Postage)

3. How To Set Up A New Testament Church
   In Your Home, By Cline Paden
        16 page booklet   .25
   (Please send stamped envelope with your address)

Write To The Publisher

Star Bible Publications, Inc.
7120 Burns Street
Fort Worth, Texas 76118

817/284-0521   817/589-1621